JOYFUL NOEL

Rediscovering Classic Christmas Hymns and Carols

25

ADVENT HYMNS
DAILY DEVOTIONALS
AND PRAYERS

POLMARRON
PRESS

An independent Publisher bringing you books everyone will want to read.

We like being small, this means our fantastic writers and editors can create the books they love and you will want to read. Our focus is non-fiction, and you'll find our books in both paperback and eBook formats.

We've got a book club too, join below (dogs welcome).

Joyful Noel

Rediscovering Classic Christmas Carols
25 Advent Hymns with Daily Devotionals
A short history of 25 Seasonal Hymns
Unwrapping the Story of Each Carol
Morning and Evening Prayers and Devotions

John Williamson

CONTENTS

INTRODUCTION

There's a certain magic that fills the air when Christmas carols are sung. The melodies, both haunting and joyful, echo through time, carrying with them stories of yesteryears and hopes for tomorrow. They're more than just songs; they're timeless narratives wrapped in harmony and rhythm. Consider this, every Christmas carol you've ever hummed or sung has a rich history behind it. Each one was born out of unique circumstances, inspired by deep faith, profound love, or sheer joy. These carols have traveled through centuries, surviving wars and revolutions, evolving with changing cultures and societies.

Take 'Silent Night', for instance. This beloved carol was composed in 1818 by Franz Xaver Gruber to lyrics by Joseph Mohr in the small town of Oberndorf bei Salzburg, Austria. It was declared an intangible cultural heritage by UNESCO in 2011. Or 'Hark! The Herald Angels Sing', originally written by Charles Wesley in 1739, it underwent several modifications before settling into the version we know today. These aren't just songs; they're living pieces of history that continue to inspire and uplift millions around the globe every holiday season.

In this book, you'll find the complete version of 25 classic Christmas carols. You'll discover how they came to be and how they've evolved over time. Each chapter focusses on one carol, and like unwrapping a cherished Christmas gift on Christmas morning, we unveil the stories running through them. It's a joyous exploration of imagination, faith, history, and the power of music.

Each hymn is also followed by daily devotionals inspired by its message, designed to help you reflect on the deeper meanings behind these familiar tunes, and perhaps find new insights within their lyrics. These morning and evening prayers are related to each carol's theme, and created to help you start and end your day with a sense of peace and purpose. So, let's pull back the curtain on these timeless hymns and discover the treasures of celebration and faith hidden within their music together.

1
Angels from the Realms of Glory

Angels from the realms of glory,
Wing your flight o'er all the earth;
Ye who sang creation's story,
Now proclaim Messiah's birth:
Come and worship,
Come and worship,
Worship Christ, the newborn King!

Shepherds, in the fields abiding,
Watching o'er your flocks by night,
God with man is now residing,
Yonder shines the infant Light;
Come and worship,
Come and worship,
Worship Christ, the newborn King!

Sages, leave your contemplations,
Brighter visions beam afar;
Seek the great desire of nations,
Ye have seen His natal star;
Come and worship,
Come and worship,
Worship Christ, the newborn King!

Saints before the altar bending,
Watching long in hope and fear,
Suddenly the Lord, descending,
In His temple shall appear:
Come and worship,
Come and worship,
Worship Christ, the newborn King!

A short history

"Angels from the Realms of Glory" is a Christmas carol with a rich history and theological depth. The lyrics were penned by Scottish poet James Montgomery and were first published in 1816. Montgomery, born in 1771, was a prolific hymn writer and newspaper editor, known for his contributions to hymnody and his work as an abolitionist.

The hymn's lyrics, set to the tune "Regent Square" composed by Henry Smart, invite us to join the heavenly chorus in celebrating the birth of Jesus. The carol focuses on the angelic proclamation to the shepherds in Luke 2:8-15, portraying the majestic scene of angels heralding the arrival of the Saviour

This jubilant hymn emphasises the universal significance of Christ's birth, calling on people to worship the newborn King. It has been embraced by various Christian denominations and is often sung during the Christmas season as an expression of adoration for the Christ-child.

The enduring appeal of "Angels from the Realms of Glory" lies not only in its melodic beauty but also in its timeless message, which continues to resonate with people worldwide. This hymn stands as a testament to James Montgomery's poetic prowess and his ability to craft verses that capture the wonder and joy of the Christmas story.

Unwrapping the story

The lyrics of this hymn invite readers to envision the celestial spectacle that unfolded on the night of Christ's birth, painting a vivid scene where angels descend from heaven to proclaim the arrival of the newborn King.

The story unfolds against the backdrop of Bethlehem. Angels beckon shepherds to hasten to Bethlehem and witness this momentous event unfolding on Earth. Echoing the biblical account found in Luke where an angelic host announces the birth of Jesus to the shepherds in the fields.

As the angels descend the hymn captures the essence of their proclamation: "Come and worship, come and worship, worship Christ, the newborn King!" This refrain becomes a rhythmic and joyful invitation for all to come and worship the newborn King, recognizing the profound implications of the Incarnation for humanity.

In essence, the hymn serves as a harmonious blend of celestial praise and earthly rejoicing, connecting people with the awe-inspiring message of Christmas. It beckons us to respond with adoration and wonder, just as the shepherds did on that holy night.

Morning Devotion

As a new day begins I think of the image of angels announcing Jesus' birth. Let it fill me with awe and wonder. As I go about my day, help me pause and worship and in the midst of daily tasks. Let me feel the presence of something extraordinary, and the hymn's words guide my focus to the true meaning of Christmas.

Evening Devotion

As the night falls let me find peace in the timeless story of Jesus' birth, and the image of angels and shepherds as a symbol of revelation and response. I offer my gratitude and worship to Christ, the newborn King. In the quiet of the night, let this hymn become a joyful prayer as I recognise how Christmas transforms my life.

2
Angels We Have Heard on High

Angels we have heard on high,
Sweetly singing o'er the plains,
And the mountains in reply
Echoing their joyous strains.

Gloria, in excelsis Deo!
Gloria, in excelsis Deo!

Shepherds, why this jubilee?
Why your joyous strains prolong?
What the gladsome tidings be
which inspire your heav'nly song?

Gloria, in excelsis Deo!
Gloria, in excelsis Deo!

Come to Bethlehem and see
Him whose birth the angels sing;
Come, adore on bended knee
Christ the Lord, the new-born King.

Gloria, in excelsis Deo!
Gloria, in excelsis Deo!

See Him in a manger laid,
Jesus, Lord of heav'n and earth!
Mary, Joseph, lend your aid,
Sing with us our Saviour's birth.

Gloria, in excelsis Deo!
Gloria, in excelsis Deo!

A brief history

"Angels We Have Heard on High" originates from a traditional French carol titled "Les Anges dans nos campagnes." This festive hymn found its way into English-speaking traditions through the translation efforts of James Chadwick in the mid-19th century. The carol is steeped in the biblical story of the angels announcing the birth of Jesus to the humble shepherds in Bethlehem.

With roots in French folk culture, the hymn's joyous melody mirrors the exuberance of the angels' proclamation. The refrain, "Gloria in excelsis Deo," serves as the heart of the hymn, echoing the resounding praise offered by the heavenly hosts, which translates to "Glory to God in the highest." This refrain has become synonymous with the Christmas season, capturing the essence of worship and adoration of the Nativity.

The enduring popularity of this carol lies not only in its musical celebration, but also its ability to transport listeners to the pastoral scene described in the Gospel of Luke. It invites people to join the shepherds in marvelling at the heavenly announcement and to respond with awe and praise for the newborn King.

Unwrapping the story

"Angels We Have Heard on High" is a joyful celebration of Christ's birth, resonating with a passion to make us feel like the heavens are singing. Each verse is a journey through the story of angelic voices echoing from the heavens, inviting us to join their chorus of awe and worship.

As the shepherds paused, captivated by the sweet melodies of angels on the plains, the hymn encourages us to stop and appreciate life's simple moments amidst the seasonal rush. Standing as a witness to the proclamation, the mountains respond with echoes of joy that ripple through valleys. As we navigate through life, the hymn prompts us to witness and find joy in gratitude, kindness, and love in our own journey.

The refrain, "Gloria in excelsis Deo," resounds with the glory of God. As the hymn calls us to join the heavenly chorus, proclaiming the Saviour's birth. It inspires everyone to embrace and share the joy of angels.

In essence, "Angels We Have Heard on High" is more than just a hymn. It's a guide to slowing down, finding joy in simplicity and joining a chorus of joy and love at Christmas.

Morning Reflection

As I start this day, I reflect on the joyous celebration of Advent with a reminder that each day is filled with extraordinary moments. Help me, like the shepherds, pause and find celebration in the simple moments of life, amidst the rush and noise. Let gratitude, kindness, and love echo through my day, spreading joy and celebration to others.

Evening Reflection

As the day winds down and I settle for the night, I think of the eternal stillness of the mountains since the dawn of creation. In the quiet of the evening, let my life be witness to moments of joy that ripple through the valleys of each day. I join the heavenly chorus in proclaiming the joy of Christ's birth. Let the anthem of angels remind me of the simple and profound pleasures found in each day.

3
Away in a Manger

Away in a manger,
No crib for His bed
The little Lord Jesus
Laid down His sweet head

The stars in the bright sky
Looked down where He lay
The little Lord Jesus
Asleep on the hay

The cattle are lowing
The poor Baby wakes
But little Lord Jesus
No crying He makes

I love Thee, Lord Jesus
Look down from the sky
And stay by my side,
'Til morning is nigh.

Be near me, Lord Jesus,
I ask Thee to stay
Close by me forever
And love me I pray

Bless all the dear children
In Thy tender care
And take us to heaven
To live with Thee there.

A brief history

"Away in a Manger" is a beloved Christmas carol commonly known for its sweet and simple portrayal of the Nativity scene. Focusing on the infant Jesus in a manger, surrounded by Mary and Joseph, each verse captures various elements of the Christmas story as told in the Gospels of Matthew and Luke.

Uncertainty surrounds the origins of the hymn, and it's often attributed to various sources. However, the lyrics are commonly thought to have originated in the United States in the late 19th century. Historically the hymn is often associated with the American Lutheran community. It first appeared in print in the late 19th century and lyrics have been attributed to various authors, including Martin Luther and various American hymn writers. However, no conclusive evidence links it to any particular author. It's likely that the hymn developed over time with contributions from different sources.

Over the years this hymn gained popularity through church hymnals and Sunday schools, becoming a cherished part of celebrations. The gentle and peaceful lyrics make it a favourite for children and adults alike. Despite the uncertainty surrounding its origins, "Away in a Manger" continues to be a timeless and cherished part of the Christmas musical tradition. It has been recorded by numerous artists and is sung in various settings during the holiday season around the world.

Unwrapping the story

This cherished hymn invites us to step into the tender scene of the first Christmas, where simplicity and profound love converge. Picture the humble stable in Bethlehem where the miraculous birth of Jesus Christ unfolds. The soft glow of starlight and the quiet of the night setting the stage for this divine moment.

The core of this narrative immerses us in the gentle moments where Mary cradles her newborn son with warmth and love. Each verse paints a picture of the unassuming Nativity story, highlighting the peace that surrounded the infant Jesus. The unpretentious melody encourages us to pause, express gratitude, and discover joy in life's modest moments - a timeless story echoing themes of love and humility.

As we journey through each verse, we find ourselves not just observers, but participants in the unfolding story of Christmas. We are prompted to embrace the simplicity of this divine moment, to appreciate the beauty in the ordinary, and to find solace in the profound love symbolised by the newborn King. It's an invitation to reflect on the enduring message of hope, peace, and the boundless love encapsulated in the humble setting of Bethlehem.

In essence, "Away in a Manger" becomes a gentle guide, urging us to slow down and embrace the timeless truths embedded in the Christmas narrative. It's an unadorned yet poignant melody that resonates with the beauty of love and the profound event that is the Saviour's birth.

Morning Devotion

As the morning sun graces the horizon, I turn my thoughts to the serene scene of Bethlehem, where the Christ child lay in a manger. With soft melodies in my heart I begin my day in quiet reflection. Just as the stars looked down upon that sacred moment, may your light guide me today. As I step into the day, help me carry simplicity and humility of my heart.

Evening Devotion

As the day gently fades into evening, I return to the Nativity, the stars overhead, and the peace that the birth of Jesus Christ brought to the world. I offer my gratitude and reflections in the quiet moments before rest. In the silence at the end of day I lay down before you any anxieties or regrets, and trust in your arms to carry me gently through the night.

4
Come, Thou Long Expected Jesus

Come, Thou long expected Jesus
Born to set Thy people free;
From our fears and sins release us,
Let us find our rest in Thee.
Israel's Strength and Consolation,
Hope of all the earth Thou art;
Dear Desire of every nation,
Joy of every longing heart.

Born Thy people to deliver,
Born a child and yet a King,
Born to reign in us forever,
Now Thy gracious kingdom bring.
By Thine own eternal Spirit
Rule in all our hearts alone;
By Thine all sufficient merit,
Raise us to Thy glorious throne.

A brief history

"Come Thou Long Expected Jesus" was penned by Charles Wesley, one of the founders of the Methodist movement, around 1744. Inspired by his deep theological reflections, the hymn reflects the anticipation of the Messiah's arrival, combining the themes of Advent, prophecy, and the hope of redemption. His hymn-writing prowess, coupled with a deep commitment to theological reflection, has produced many enduring compositions.

The hymn beautifully encapsulates the spirit of Advent, embodying the collective anticipation for the Messiah's imminent arrival. Drawing from the themes of prophecy and the redemptive hope found in Jesus, Wesley's verses convey a profound yearning that resonates across generations.

Wesley's impact on hymnody extends beyond this particular composition, as he penned thousands of hymns during his lifetime. His hymns, characterised by rich theology and emotive expression, have left an indelible mark on Christian worship. "Come Thou Long Expected Jesus" remains a cherished component of Advent traditions, continuing to inspire people to reflect on the anticipation and hope embedded in the Christmas story.

Unwrapping the story

"Come, Thou Long Expected Jesus" weaves together anticipation and hope, resonating with the heartfelt longing for the arrival of the Messiah. Encapsulating the essence of the Advent season, it draws us into a narrative that spans the ages, and echoes the collective yearning of generations for the fulfilment of God's promise.

The hymn opens with a poignant plea for Jesus to come and set His people free from the shackles of sin and despair. It taps into the prophetic anticipation found in the Old Testament, where promises of a Saviour reverberate throughout the pages of Scripture. The imagery evokes a sense of longing, as the hymn articulates the deep desire for the dawn of redemption.

As the verses unfold, the hymn traces the redemptive arc of God's plan, acknowledging Jesus as the hope of all nations. It alludes to various Messianic prophecies, underscoring the significance of Jesus' birth as the realisation of divine promises. The hymn becomes a poignant reminder that, in the birth of his son, God's plan takes a tangible, human form.

The refrain, "Born Thy people to deliver, born a child and yet a King," captures the paradoxical nature of Christ's Advent - a humble birth that carries cosmic implications. Going beyond historical contexts, the hymn makes the narrative of Christ's arrival a personal and communal experience. It speaks to the universal human condition, acknowledging the world's brokenness while pointing to the hope found in Christ's redemptive work. The hymn becomes a timeless expression of faith, resonating with the Advent theme of longing and expectation.

Morning Prayer

As I welcome the morning light, I turn my hearts to the anticipation embedded in "Come Thou Long Expected Jesus." Lord, help me embrace the hope and promise of your coming. May my days be filled with the expectation of your presence, and may I find comfort in the assurance of your redemption.

Evening Prayer

As the evening falls, we reflect on the day's journey, mindful of the yearning expressed in "Come Thou Long Expected Jesus." Lord, as we rest, let the echoes of hope and anticipation linger in our hearts. Grant us a peaceful night, knowing that you are the fulfilment of our deepest longings.

5
Deck the Halls

Deck the halls with boughs of holly,
Fa la la la la, la la la.
'Tis the season to be jolly,
Fa la la la la, la la la.
Don we now our gay apparel,
Fa la la la la, la la la.
Troll the ancient Yuletide carol,
Fa la la la la, la la la.

See the blazing Yule before us,
Fa la la la la, la la la.
Strike the harp and join the chorus,
Fa la la la la, la la la.
Follow me in merry measure,
Fa la la la la, la la la.
While I tell of Yuletide treasure,
Fa la la la la, la la la.

Fast away the old year passes,
Fa la la la la, la la la.
Hail the new, ye lads and lasses,
Fa la la la la, la la la.
Sing we joyous all together,
Fa la la la la, la la la.

Heedless of the wind and weather,
Fa la la la la, la la la.

A brief history

"Deck the Halls" is a traditional Welsh carol with a melody dating back to the 16th century. Its English lyrics, penned by Thomas Oliphant and first published in 1862. The carol exuberantly invites everyone to join in holiday festivities, encouraging the decking of surroundings with holly and embracing the merriment of the season. The famous "fa-la-la-la-la" refrain adds a playful and lighthearted touch to the song.

The use of holly in "Deck the Halls" is not merely decorative; it carries deep symbolic significance rooted in both Christian and pagan traditions. Holly, an evergreen plant, symbolises enduring life and hope, as its vibrant green leaves persist even in winter. The thorny leaves represent the crown of thorns worn by Jesus during the crucifixion, while the red berries symbolise drops of blood, connecting the carol to Christian themes of hope, sacrifice, and renewal.

Beyond its Christian symbolism, holly has held significance in pagan traditions, associated with protective qualities and integrated into winter solstice celebrations. The integration of holly in the carol weaves together diverse cultural and religious threads, creating a rich tapestry of meaning within the joyful and communal spirit of the season.

Unwrapping the story

This festive hymn encapsulates the joy and merriment of the Christmas season. Its lively and rhythmic melody sets the stage for a jubilant celebration, inviting everyone to participate in the festivities.

Beginning with the iconic call to "Deck the halls with boughs of holly," this lively directive immediately establishes a festive atmosphere, urging people to adorn their surroundings with traditional Christmas greenery. The use of holly, a symbol of goodwill and joy, adds a touch of nature to the seasonal decorations.

The repetition of the fa-la-la refrain adds a playful and communal element to the hymn. It's as if the song itself is inviting everyone to join in the merrymaking, fostering a sense of togetherness and unity.

The second verse introduces the Yuletide carol, emphasising the joy of singing together during this special time of year. The mention of the ancient Yuletide carol connects the contemporary celebration to age-old traditions, creating a sense of continuity and shared history through merrymaking and revelry. The phrase "troll the ancient Yuletide carol" invites people to embrace the festive spirit with cheerful abandon. The term "troll" here doesn't refer to internet mischief but instead implies singing or joyfully participating in a merry manner.

In essence, "Deck the Halls" becomes a musical invitation to take part in traditions of the Christmas season. It celebrates the communal spirit of decorating homes, singing carols, and embracing the festive atmosphere.

Morning Devotional

As the morning sun rises, I come before You, grateful for a new day, inspired by the festive spirit of "Deck the Halls." Help me adorn my day with acts of kindness, joy, and a melody of gratitude, embracing the enduring hope symbolised by holly. Guide my interactions to spread goodwill, and may the day resonate with a cheerful and merry refrain.

Evening Devotional

As night falls, I reflect on the playful rhythms of "Deck the Halls." The communal spirit in its melodies echoes the day's togetherness. I'm thankful for the enduring hope represented by holly, reminding me of Your constant love. In the quiet of the night, let the joyous celebration of the season linger, creating a melody of peace. Thank You for the festive unity and the enduring spirit of hope.

6
Ding Dong Merrily on High

Ding dong, merrily on high!
In heav'n the bells are ringing;
Ding dong, verily the sky
Is riv'n with angel singing.

Gloria, hosannah in excelsis!
Gloria, hosannah in excelsis!

E'en so here below,
Let steeple bells be swungen,
And io, io, io,
By priest and people sungen.

Gloria, hosannah in excelsis!
Gloria, hosannah in excelsis!

Pray ye dutifully prime
Your matin chime, ye ringers;
May ye beautifully rhyme
Your evetime song, ye singers.

Gloria, hosannah in excelsis!
Gloria, hosannah in excelsis!

A brief history

"Ding Dong Merrily on High" is a festive gem with origins deeply rooted in French and English musical traditions. The melody, dating back to the 16th century, emanates from the French dance piece "Branle de l'Official." This lively and rhythmic tune found its way into the hearts of celebrants, becoming synonymous with the joyous atmosphere of Christmas.

In the 19th century, the English lyrics we now associate with the carol were crafted by George Ratcliffe Woodward. A noteworthy figure, Woodward was not only a skilled musician but also a scholar and Anglican clergyman. His background allowed him to infuse the carol with a thoughtful blend of jubilation and reverence.

The hymn's lyrics go beyond a mere celebration of the season; they beautifully capture the essence of Christmas with a focus on the ringing of bells. These bells, symbolising merriment and jubilation, become a central theme, creating a sensory experience that invites worshippers and carollers alike to immerse themselves in the festive spirit.

Moreover, "Ding Dong Merrily on High" draws inspiration from the biblical narrative of the angels' proclamation of Christ's birth. This connection with the angelic announcement adds a layer of sacredness to the carol, making it not only a jubilant expression of Christmas cheer but also a testament to the divine significance of the season.

The hymn acts as a musical invitation, encouraging everyone to join in this exultant chorus of praise. Its enduring popularity and widespread use in Christmas celebrations worldwide attest to its timeless appeal and its ability to resonate with the collective joy and reverence associated with the birth of Christ.

Unwrapping the Story

"Ding Dong Merrily on High" unfolds as a jubilant celebration, echoing the joyous sounds of Christmas. The narrative sweeps singers and listeners into the festive atmosphere, capturing the merriment of the holiday season. The hymn invites us to embrace the festive bells ringing together, symbolising unity and the shared happiness of Christmas.

Exploring themes of communal celebration, "Ding Dong Merrily on High" underscores the universal spirit of Christmas. The vibrant imagery of bells ringing high in the heavens creates a sense of harmony and togetherness. The hymn encourages people to revel in the collective joy and spread the message of Christmas cheer.

In a modern retelling, imagine a town coming together to decorate the streets with lights and ornaments. Families and friends join in the festivities, exchanging laughter and creating memories. The ringing bells become a symbol of shared happiness, calling everyone to unite in the celebration of love, goodwill, and the birth of Christ.

Morning Prayer

As the morning sun rises, let our hearts resonate with the joyous echoes of Christmas. May we embrace the shared celebration, finding connection and unity with those around us. Lord, fill our day with the spirit of love and togetherness as we reflect the joy of your birth.

Evening Prayer

As the evening bells chime, we thank you, Lord, for the day's shared moments of happiness and celebration. May the echoes of love linger in our hearts, reminding us of the unity found in the Christmas season. Bless our night with peace and gratitude for the gift of togetherness.

7

God Rest Ye Merry Gentlemen

God rest ye merry, gentlemen
Let nothing you dismay
Remember, Christ, our Saviour
Was born on Christmas day
To save us all from Satan's power
When we were gone astray
O tidings of comfort and joy,
Comfort and joy
O tidings of comfort and joy

In Bethlehem, in Israel,
This blessed Babe was born
And laid within a manger
Upon this blessed morn
The which His Mother Mary
Did nothing take in scorn
O tidings of comfort and joy,
Comfort and joy
O tidings of comfort and joy

From God our Heavenly Father
A blessed Angel came;
And unto certain Shepherds
Brought tidings of the same:

How that in Bethlehem was born
The Son of God by Name.
O tidings of comfort and joy,
Comfort and joy
O tidings of comfort and joy

"Fear not then," said the Angel,
"Let nothing you affright,
This day is born a Saviour
Of a pure Virgin bright,
To free all those who trust in Him
From Satan's power and might."
O tidings of comfort and joy,
Comfort and joy
O tidings of comfort and joy

The shepherds at those tidings
Rejoiced much in mind,
And left their flocks a-feeding
In tempest, storm and wind:
And went to Bethlehem straightway
The Son of God to find.
O tidings of comfort and joy,
Comfort and joy
O tidings of comfort and joy

And when they came to Bethlehem
Where our dear Saviour lay,
They found Him in a manger,
Where oxen feed on hay;
His Mother Mary kneeling down,
Unto the Lord did pray.
O tidings of comfort and joy,

Comfort and joy
O tidings of comfort and joy

Now to the Lord sing praises,
All you within this place,
And with true love and brotherhood
Each other now embrace;
This holy tide of Christmas
All other doth deface.
O tidings of comfort and joy,
Comfort and joy
O tidings of comfort and joy.

A brief history

Believed to trace its lyrical origins back to the 18th century, "God Rest Ye Merry, Gentlemen" is a traditional English Christmas carol embodying the festive spirit with deep historical roots.

The melody accompanying the lyrics is also of ancient origin, further enhancing the carol's timeless and traditional allure. Rooted in the vast English musical heritage, the tune has gracefully moved through time, becoming an integral part of Yuletide celebrations.

At its core, the hymn serves as a messenger of the good news surrounding the birth of Christ. It encourages not only festive celebration but also a profound sense of comfort and joy. The story woven into the lyrics becomes a proclamation of the Advent of Jesus. It invites worshipers and carollers alike to immerse themselves in the jubilation of Christ's birth, fostering an atmosphere of comfort, joy, and the message of salvation that echoes through the ages.

Unwrapping the story

"God Rest Ye Merry, Gentlemen" is a Christmas hymn that conveys a message of comfort, joy, and reassurance. Its traditional melody and rich lyrics have made it a beloved part of the holiday season, resonating with themes of hope and goodwill.

It begins with the directive, "God rest ye merry, gentlemen." This opening phrase may be a bit archaic in its language, but its essence is a wish for God's restful peace upon those who hear the message. The term "merry" in this context refers to joy and the sense of well-being and contentment, transforming it into an expression of happiness and celebration.

The next line encourages listeners not to be dismayed, connecting the message directly to the timeless Christmas story. It's an assurance that, despite challenges, the message of Christmas brings great joy and consolation. The hymn invites people to approach the season with a sense of peace and assurance.

The refrain, "O tidings of comfort and joy," serves as a jubilant proclamation. It declares that the message of Christmas is not only about the birth of Christ but also about the comfort and happiness that this event brings. The repetition of this refrain emphasises the core themes of the hymn.

The second verse tells the story of the Saviour's birth, and the divine nature of the event. It encourages us to trust in God's plan and find comfort in the knowledge that Christ was born for our salvation. The carol's story weaves together a sense of awe and celebration, recognizing the profound impact of this moment.

As the verses progress, they maintain a sense of urgency and exhortation. The call to "let nothing you dismay" is a reminder to hold on to the message of Christmas despite life's challenges. It encourages us to find solace and joy in the eternal significance of Christ's birth.

In summary, "God Rest Ye Merry, Gentlemen" is a timeless hymn that invites people to embrace the comfort and joy offered by the Christmas message. It combines a wish for God's restful peace with a jubilant proclamation of the good news, making it a heartening and uplifting anthem for the holiday season.

Morning Devotion

As the morning sun rises, I come before You, inspired by the timeless message of "God Rest Ye Merry, Gentlemen." May Your restful peace and joy accompany me throughout this day, granting strength to face challenges with unwavering trust. As I navigate the day's journey, let the comfort and joy of the Christmas message echo in my heart, bringing solace in moments of dismay.

Evening Devotion

As night falls, I reflect on the day, grateful for the comfort and joy of life. In moments of challenge, I sought comfort and solace, and in moments of joy I celebrated the jubilant message of Christmas. Thank You for the reassurance and peace that accompany Your good news.

8
Good King Wenceslas

Good King Wenceslas looked out
On the feast of Stephen
When the snow lay round about
Deep and crisp and even
Brightly shone the moon that night
Though the frost was cruel
When a poor man came in sight
Gath'ring winter fuel

"Hither, page, and stand by me
If thou know'st it, telling
Yonder peasant, who is he?
Where and what his dwelling?"
"Sire, he lives a good league hence
Underneath the mountain
Right against the forest fence
By Saint Agnes' fountain."

"Bring me flesh and bring me wine
Bring me pine logs hither
Thou and I will see him dine
When we bear him thither."
Page and monarch forth they went
Forth they went together

Through the rude wind's wild lament
And the bitter weather

"Sire, the night is darker now
And the wind blows stronger
Fails my heart, I know not how,
I can go no longer."
"Mark my footsteps, my good page
Tread thou in them boldly
Thou shalt find the winter's rage
Freeze thy blood less coldly."

In his master's steps he trod
Where the snow lay dinted
Heat was in the very sod
Which the Saint had printed
Therefore, Christian men, be sure
Wealth or rank possessing
Ye who now will bless the poor
Shall yourselves find blessing.

A brief history

"Good King Wenceslas" is a Christmas carol that has its roots in both historical and musical traditions, celebrating the virtues of generosity, kindness, and compassion. Its enduring appeal lies in its connection to both the historical figure of Wenceslas I and the universal themes of goodwill and charity.

The hymn is inspired by the historical figure of Wenceslas I, also known as Saint Wenceslaus, a 10th-century Duke of Bohemia. He is revered as a martyr and saint in the Christian tradition, known for his piety, kindness, and efforts to spread Christianity in Bohemia, now part of the Czech Republic. The carol is closely tied to the Feast of Stephen, celebrated on December 26th in Western Christianity, commemorating Saint Stephen, the first Christian martyr. The connection to this feast adds a religious context to the song.

The lyrics of "Good King Wenceslas" were written by John Mason Neale in the 19th century. Neale was a hymn writer and scholar who contributed significantly to English hymnody. He had a deep appreciation for medieval literature and culture, which is evident in the language and style of the lyrics. The melody of "Good King Wenceslas" is based on a 13th-century spring carol called "Tempus adest floridum" (The Time is Near for Flowering). The adaptation of an existing melody from the medieval period contributes to the carol's historic and traditional feel. Over the years, the carol has been arranged and recorded by various artists and ensembles, contributing to its popularity. The combination of a memorable melody and lyrics with a meaningful narrative has made it a favourite during the Christmas season.

Unwrapping the story

"Good King Wenceslas" tells the story of a generous Duke who, on the Feast of Stephen (the day after Christmas), looks out and sees a poor man gathering winter fuel. Filled with empathy he decides to take action, and accompanied by his page braves a severe winter storm to provide aid. The act of venturing out into the harsh weather to help someone in need reflects themes of generosity, kindness, and Christian virtues. The deep sense of caring and concern for those less fortunate, encapsulates the essence of Christmas in the spirit and act of compassion and giving.

The lyrics describe the physical challenges faced by the Duke and his page as they trudge through the snow. This vivid imagery adds a layer of realism to the narrative, emphasising the sacrifice and effort required to practice goodwill. The king's determination to serve others in need becomes a powerful example of Christian virtues.

The refrain reinforces the moral of the story: "Therefore, Christian men, be sure. Wealth or rank possessing. Ye who now will bless the poor. Shall yourselves find blessing." This call to action encourages people not only to appreciate the Duke's generosity but also to embody the seasonal spirit by extending kindness to those in need.

In conclusion, "Good King Wenceslas" is more than just a delightful Christmas tune. It weaves a tale of compassion, sacrifice, and the joy found in helping others. The hymn's enduring appeal lies in its ability to convey the timeless message that, especially during the Christmas season, acts of kindness and generosity can bring warmth and light to the lives of those less fortunate.

Morning Reflection

As the morning light breaks may I find inspiration in this timeless story and approach this day with the same compassion and generosity displayed, reaching out to those in need. Grant me the strength to face challenges and the wisdom to extend kindness. In my actions let the spirit of giving and goodwill shine brightly.

Evening Reflection

As the day comes to a close, I reflect on the messages of "Good King Wenceslas." The actions of compassion and selflessness resonates in my heart. In the moments where I could extend a helping hand, may I embody the Christmas spirit of generosity. Thank you for the reminder that, through acts of kindness, we find blessings for ourselves and others.

9
Hark! The Herald Angels Sing

Hark the herald angels sing
"Glory to the newborn King!
Peace on earth and mercy mild
God and sinners reconciled"
Joyful, all ye nations rise
Join the triumph of the skies
With the angelic host proclaim:
"Christ is born in Bethlehem"

Hark! The herald angels sing
"Glory to the newborn King!"

Christ by highest heav'n adored
Christ the everlasting Lord!
Late in time behold Him come
Offspring of a Virgin's womb
Veiled in flesh the Godhead see
Hail the incarnate Deity
Pleased as man with man to dwell
Jesus, our Emmanuel

Hark! The herald angels sing
"Glory to the newborn King!"

Hail the heav'n-born Prince of Peace!
Hail the Son of Righteousness!
Light and life to all He brings
Ris'n with healing in His wings
Mild He lays His glory by
Born that man no more may die
Born to raise the sons of earth
Born to give them second birth

Hark! The herald angels sing
"Glory to the newborn King!"

A brief history

"Hark! The Herald Angels Sing" has its origins in the collaboration of three significant figures in Christian hymnody: Charles Wesley, George Whitefield, and Felix Mendelssohn. The lyrics were penned by Charles Wesley in 1739, one of the founders of the Methodist movement.

Originally written as part of a collection of hymns for the celebration of the Nativity of Christ, Wesley's words were titled "Hymn for Christmas-Day" and later adapted to become the well-known carol.

The adaptation of Wesley's lyrics into the hymn we know today is credited to George Whitefield, a preacher closely associated with the Methodist movement. Whitefield adjusted some of the verses to create a more structured hymn. Finally, the melody of the hymn is based on a cantata by Felix Mendelssohn, a German composer.

The melody was adapted by William H. Cummings and paired with Wesley's lyrics, creating the familiar tune we sing today. The hymn has become a classic Christmas carol, known for its triumphant proclamation of the birth of Christ and the joyous announcement by the herald angels.

Unwrapping the story

"Hark! The Herald Angels Sing" is a jubilant Christmas hymn proclaiming the birth of Jesus Christ through the angels' announcement to the shepherds, as recorded in the Gospel of Luke.

Opening with an exuberant call to attention, this introduction sets the tone of celebration of a momentous event - the birth of the King bringing peace and reconciliation between God and humanity.

The hymn goes on to describe the attributes of the newborn King, Jesus, as the "Son of Righteousness" who brings light and life to a world in darkness. The reference to the "everlasting Lord" highlights the divinity of the infant born in Bethlehem, weaving together theological truths about Christ's nature and purpose.

The second verse continues the story and the miraculous nature of the Incarnation. It reflects on Christ's descent from heaven to earth, taking on human form to redeem fallen humanity. The imagery of angels singing captures the mystery and wonder of the Christmas story.

The hymn's chorus reaffirms the angelic proclamation with a triumphant declaration. Each line encapsulating the hope and salvation brought by the birth of Jesus, emphasising His role as the Prince of Peace and the source of healing.

"Hark! The Herald Angels Sing" is a resounding Advent anthem that encapsulates the joy, wonder, and theological significance of the Christmas story. It invites worshipers to join the heavenly chorus in celebrating the arrival of the newborn King, recognizing Jesus as the embodiment of peace, righteousness, and divine grace.

Morning Devotion

As the morning sun rises, I am filled with the triumphant spirit of "Hark! The Herald Angels Sing." Let my heart resonate with the joyous proclamation of the angels. May I carry the message of peace and hope throughout this day, reflecting the light of Christ in my actions as I celebrate the birth of my Saviour.

Evening Reflection

As the day ends I reflect on joy and wonder of the angels' proclamation. In the quiet of this evening, let the words of this hymn be a reminder of the divine peace brought by the newborn King. May His presence continue to illuminate my path, and may the echoes of heavenly praise fill my heart with gratitude.

10
In the Bleak Midwinter

In the bleak midwinter
Frosty wind made moan,
Earth stood hard as iron,
Water like a stone:
Snow had fallen,
Snow on snow, snow on snow,
In the bleak midwinter,
Long ago.

Our God, heaven cannot hold him,
Nor earth sustain;
Heaven and earth shall flee away
When he comes to reign:
In the bleak midwinter
A stable place sufficed
The Lord God Almighty,
Jesus Christ.

Enough for him whom cherubim
Worship night and day,
A breastful of milk
And a mangerful of hay:
Enough for him
Whom angels fall down before,

The ox and ass and camel
Which adore.

Angels and archangels
May have gathered there,
Cherubim and seraphim
Thronged the air,
But only his mother,
In her maiden bliss,
Worshiped the Beloved
With a kiss.

What can I give him,
Poor as I am?
If I were a shepherd,
I would bring a lamb,
If I were a wise man
I would do my part,
Yet what I can I give him,
Give my heart.

A brief history

"In the Bleak Midwinter" is a poignant Christmas carol rooted in a poem by esteemed English poet Christina Rossetti, first published in 1872. However, it wasn't until 1906 that the renowned British composer and teacher Gustav Holst created the iconic musical adaptation that would elevate the poem to the status of a beloved hymn. Holst, well-known for his orchestral masterpiece "The Planets," applied his musical genius to Rossetti's verses, crafting a hauntingly beautiful melody that perfectly complements the reflective and contemplative nature of the lyrics.

Holst's adaptation skilfully portrays the humble and austere conditions surrounding the birth of Christ, emphasising the contrast between the harsh external environment and the warmth of the divine event. Despite the bleakness depicted in the verses, "In the Bleak Midwinter" transforms into a powerful reflection on the capacity for love and devotion directed towards the Christ child. It becomes a meditation on the profound meaning of Christmas, transcending the physical harshness of winter to focus on the spiritual depth of the Nativity.

The emotional power of the hymn lies in its ability to capture the duality of the season, acknowledging external challenges while elevating the story to a higher place of contemplation. "In the Bleak Midwinter" endures not only for its lyrical beauty but also for the brilliant musical adaptation by Gustav Holst, which has become the most well-known and widely performed version of the hymn.

Holst's contribution has ensured that the carol continues to evoke a profound emotional response, inviting reflection on enduring themes of love, devotion, and the sacredness of Christmas.

Unwrapping the story

"In the Bleak Midwinter" evokes a profound sense of contemplation as it paints a vivid picture of the humble circumstances surrounding the birth of Jesus Christ. The hymn is a meditation on the stark and simple setting of the Nativity scene, emphasising the harshness of winter and the challenging conditions into which Jesus entered the world.

Captures the essence of simplicity, with Earth described as "hard as iron" and water "like a stone," the repetition of snowfall creates an image of a desolate landscape covered in layers of snow, emphasising the starkness of the midwinter environment. This serves as a metaphor for the harsh realities of life and the contrast with the warmth and hope brought by the arrival of the Christ-child.

The second verse shifts the focus to the response of those present at the manger. It prompts reflection on what gifts one might bring to honour the newborn King. This contemplation extends beyond material offerings, encouraging us to consider the deeper significance of our devotion and commitment. The refrain's query, "What can I give Him, poor as I am?" invites introspection about one's personal offering to the divine.

The hymn also explores the paradox of the incarnation in the eternal Word of God taking on the form of a vulnerable infant. This paradox is presented through the imagery of angels, archangels, cherubim, and seraphim surrounding the scene. The emphasis on Mary worshiping the baby with a kiss, highlights the intimate and human aspects of the divine moment.

As the hymn concludes, the emphasis on the simplicity of offerings persists. The final lines underscore the idea that, in the midst of personal inadequacy, the most meaningful gift one can give is the heart. This emphasis on the heart as a symbolic offering speaks to the transformative power of love and devotion, emphasising the personal and spiritual response to the significance of Christ's birth.

"In the Bleak Midwinter" serves as a profound meditation on the themes of simplicity, humility, and personal devotion in the face of the profound mystery of the incarnation.

Morning Devotion

I embrace the dawn in this quiet moment and reflect on the humble circumstances of Your birth. In the midst of life's challenges, help me find the warmth of devotion, and the transformative power of love. As I navigate this day, may the hymn's contemplative melody guide me in simplicity and humility.

Evening Reflection

In the stillness of this evening I turn to the eternal themes of simplicity, love, and devotion. May the contrast between the starkness of winter and the warmth of Your arrival inspire me to offer my heart in humble worship. In the quiet of this night, let the hymn's beauty continue to resonate within me.

11
I Saw Three Ships

I saw three ships come sailing in
On Christmas Day, on Christmas Day;
I saw three ships come sailing in
On Christmas Day in the morning.

And what was in those ships all three,
On Christmas Day, on Christmas Day?
And what was in those ships all three,
On Christmas Day in the morning?

The Virgin Mary and Christ were there,
On Christmas Day, on Christmas Day;
The Virgin Mary and Christ were there,
On Christmas Day in the morning.

Pray, wither sailed those ships all three,
On Christmas Day, on Christmas Day;
Pray, wither sailed those ships all three,
On Christmas Day in the morning?

O they sailed into Bethlehem,
On Christmas Day, on Christmas Day;
O they sailed into Bethlehem,
On Christmas Day in the morning.

And all the bells on earth shall ring,
On Christmas Day, on Christmas Day;
And all the bells on earth shall ring,
On Christmas Day in the morning.

And all the Angels in Heaven shall sing,
On Christmas Day, on Christmas Day;
And all the Angels in Heaven shall sing,
On Christmas Day in the morning.

And all the souls on earth shall sing,
On Christmas Day, on Christmas Day;
And all the souls on earth shall sing,
On Christmas Day in the morning.

Then let us all rejoice again,
On Christmas Day, on Christmas Day;
Then let us all rejoice again,
On Christmas Day in the morning.

A brief history

The origins of "I Saw Three Ships" come from a traditional English Christmas carol, whose roots go back to the 17th century. It's words and melody are also deeply embedded in the English folk music tradition. While the authorship is uncertain and the lyrics have variations, the song is generally associated with the mystery plays of the Middle Ages, where it might have been performed as part of seasonal celebrations.

The carol typically depicts the image of three ships sailing into Bethlehem. The symbolism of the ships is thought to represent the three wise men, or Magi, who journeyed to Bethlehem to visit the newborn Christ. The theme revolves around the joyous arrival of these travellers to witness the significant event of the Nativity.

As with many traditional carols, "I Saw Three Ships" has evolved over the centuries, and various versions exist. The melody and lyrics have been passed down through generations, contributing to its enduring popularity during the Christmas season. The song captures the festive spirit of Christmas, celebrating the arrival of the Magi and conveying a sense of joy and wonder associated with the birth of Jesus.

Unwrapping the story

"I Saw Three Ships" is a jubilant hymn that shares the joyful narrative of the Christmas story, capturing the essence of celebration and anticipation. This delightful carol opens with a vivid image of three ships sailing in on Christmas Day, carrying the promise of good news and festive cheer.

The hymn creates a sense of wonder and excitement as it invites people to imagine the arrival of these ships, each laden with treasures. The ships become symbolic vessels of hope, ushering in a season of joy and rejoicing. The whimsical imagery paints a picture of a journey that transcends the ordinary, heralding a special arrival that brings glad tidings to all.

As the story unfolds, the hymn weaves in references to the Nativity story, evoking scenes of shepherds and wise men who journeyed to witness the birth of the Saviour. The ships become a metaphor for the miraculous nature of Christ's Advent, emphasising the transformative power of His arrival on that holy night.

The refrain, with its lively melody, becomes a communal expression of joy and celebration. It captures the universal spirit of Christmas, inviting everyone to join in the merriment. The hymn becomes a joyful proclamation of the good news, encouraging people to participate in the festive atmosphere surrounding the birth of Christ.

"I Saw Three Ships" is more than a recounting of historical events; it is an invitation to embrace the joy and wonder of Christmas. Through its vibrant narrative and spirited lyrics and melody, the hymn encourages everyone to envision the miraculous arrival of Christ and to celebrate the profound impact of His birth on the world.

Morning Reflection

In the gentle light of Christmas morning, let us set sail into the day with hope and anticipation. As I stand on the shore of a new day, I envision the sails of three ships catching the first rays of Christmas sunlight. May this day unfold like a journey of discovery, where each moment brings treasures of laughter, kindness, and gratitude.

Evening Reflection

As the evening tide carries us towards the close of Christmas Day, let us reflect on the ships that sailed in the morning. In the quiet moments of this evening, I picture the three ships, now silhouetted against the twilight sky. May the gifts they brought - symbolic and profound - linger in our hearts. As we retire to the peace of the night, may the joy of Christmas accompany us, like stars lighting our path.

12
It Came Upon the Midnight Clear

It came upon the midnight clear,
That glorious song of old,
From angels bending near the earth,
To touch their harps of gold:
"Peace on the earth, goodwill to men
From heavens all gracious King!"
The world in solemn stillness lay
To hear the angels sing.

Still through the cloven skies they come,
With peaceful wings unfurled;
And still their heavenly music floats
O'er all the weary world:
Above its sad and lowly plains
They bend on hovering wing,
And ever o'er its Babel sounds
The blessed angels sing.

O ye beneath life's crushing load,
Whose forms are bending low,
Who toil along the climbing way
With painful steps and slow;
Look now, for glad and golden hours
Come swiftly on the wing;

Oh rest beside the weary road
And hear the angels sing.

For lo! the days are hastening on,
By prophets seen of old,
When with the ever-circling years
Shall come the time foretold,
When the new heaven and earth shall own
The Prince of Peace, their King,
And the whole world send back the song
Which now the angels sing.

A brief history

Authored by Edmund Hamilton Sears in 1849, "It Came Upon the Midnight Clear" is a hymn rooted in the religious landscape of its time. Sears, a Unitarian minister, crafted the lyrics against the backdrop of the turbulent social and political climate in the United States, with a particular focus on the Mexican-American War and the prevailing issue of slavery.

While the original context touched on these earthly concerns, Sears' primary intent was to convey a profound message of peace and goodwill inspired by the Christian story. Sears, drawing from the biblical account of angels heralding the birth of Jesus to shepherds, wove a narrative that transcended the immediate socio-political issues of the day. The hymn becomes a reflection on the divine message of peace proclaimed by the angels in contrast to the discord prevalent in the world. It serves as a reminder of the enduring relevance of the Christmas message in times of upheaval and uncertainty.

The original five stanzas of the hymn articulate a heartfelt plea for humanity to heed the angels' message, find solace in the promise of peace emanating from the birth of Jesus, and anticipate a future age characterised by harmony and spiritual richness. Sears' vision goes beyond the contemporary challenges, inviting people to reflect on the timeless themes of peace, hope, and the transformative power of the Christian message.

In essence, "It Came Upon the Midnight Clear" stands as a testament to the enduring tradition of seeking solace and hope in the midst of societal challenges. By drawing on biblical imagery and emphasising the angelic proclamation of peace, the hymn offers a timeless perspective on the divine message that transcends the specific historical concerns of its inception, resonating with people across generations.

Unwrapping the story

"It Came Upon the Midnight Clear" unfolds as a poignant reflection on the angelic proclamation of peace on that holy night. The hymn invites contemplation on the message of goodwill and tranquility delivered by celestial beings to the shepherds.

It begins with a description of the world in a state of restlessness, portraying the chaos and tumult of human affairs. It provides a stark contrast between the discord of earthly life and the serenity brought by the angels. This sets the stage for a reflection on the enduring relevance of the angels' message peace and love, even in the face of human strife and confusion.

The hymn speaks to the angelic announcement of "peace on earth, good will to men," emphasising the divine desire for harmony and benevolence among humanity. It acknowledges the disconnect between this heavenly proclamation and the persistent struggles experienced by individuals on Earth. This conflict encourages thinking about how their message goes beyond the temporary difficulties of human life.

The second verse introduces a pastoral scene with angels bending near the earth to touch their harps of gold. This imagery adds a layer of celestial beauty to the narrative, underscoring the divine intervention in the midst of human struggles. The gentle strains of the angels' music serve as a metaphor for the soothing and transformative power of the message of peace.

The hymn also encourages contemplation of us all carrying forward the angelic mission. The call to "listen to the angels' song" implies an active engagement with the divine message and an openness to its transformative influence. As it concludes, the call for "peace on earth" persists, inviting us to consider our role in realising this vision in our lives and communities, and spreading goodwill in the world

Morning Prayer

As the dawn paints the sky with a new day, I approach you with gratitude for the gift of life. In the quiet of this morning may my actions align with the promise of goodwill and love. In a world burdened by strife, I pray for a hushing of noise and a softening of hearts. Grant strength to those toiling beneath life's load and moments of rest for weary souls. As the day unfolds, may my steps contribute to peace over all the earth.

Evening Prayer

As the evening shadows fall, I turn to you in gratitude for the day's journey. In the quiet of this evening, I release the day's cares into your hands. For those bearing burdens, I lift a prayer for strength and resilience. In anticipation of glad and golden hours, fill my heart with gratitude. As I rest may the anticipation of joy refresh my spirit as I surrender to the embrace of sleep.

13
Joy to the World

Joy to the world, the Lord is come!
Let earth receive her King;
Let every heart prepare Him room,
And Heaven and nature sing,
And Heaven and nature sing,
And Heaven, and Heaven, and nature sing.

Joy to the world, the Saviour reigns!
Let men their songs employ;
While fields and floods, rocks, hills and plains
Repeat the sounding joy,
Repeat the sounding joy,
Repeat, repeat, the sounding joy.

No more let sins and sorrows grow,
Nor thorns infest the ground;
He comes to make His blessings flow
Far as the curse is found,
Far as the curse is found,
Far as, far as, the curse is found.

He rules the world with truth and grace,
And makes the nations prove
The glories of His righteousness,
And wonders of His love,
And wonders of His love,
And wonders, wonders, of His love.

A brief history

"Joy to the World" is a familiar and timeless Christmas hymn with roots deeply embedded in the religious inspiration and musical legacy of two prominent figures: Isaac Watts and George Frideric Handel.

Isaac Watts, born in 1674, was an English Christian minister, hymn writer, and theologian. He is often regarded as the "Father of English Hymnody" for his significant contributions to hymn writing. Watts sought to bring a more personal and emotional element into worship music, departing from the exclusive use of metrical psalms. His poetic talents and theological insights are evident in the lyrics of "Joy to the World."

The melody of "Joy to the World" finds its origins in George Frideric Handel's "Messiah," an oratorio composed in 1741. Handel, born in 1685 in Germany, was a prolific composer of the Baroque era. "Messiah" became one of his most celebrated works, and its triumphant and uplifting character is reflected in the melody adapted for "Joy to the World."

The collaboration between Watts and Handel is a testament to the convergence of two influential figures in hymnody and classical music. Watts penned the jubilant lyrics, drawing inspiration from Psalm 98, while Handel's composition provided the uplifting and celebratory melody that perfectly complemented Watts' verses. The adaptation of Handel's melody for "Joy to the World" resulted in a harmonious fusion of poetic brilliance and musical excellence.

"Joy to the World" was first published in Watts' collection of hymns titled "The Psalms of David: Imitated in the Language of the New Testament" in 1719. The hymn's enduring popularity and resonance can be attributed to the genius of both Watts and Handel, whose collaboration created a musical masterpiece that continues to be a cherished part of the Christmas tradition.

Unwrapping the story

"Joy to the World" can be considered a jubilant anthem of celebration, inviting people to rejoice in the arrival of the Saviour The hymn conveys a story of praise and adoration, emphasising the universal significance of Christ's birth.

Unfolding with a resounding proclamation of "joy to the world, the Lord is come!" the hymn sets a festive tone, urging people to celebrate the arrival of the long-awaited Messiah. The narrative here centres on the anticipation and fulfilment of the promise of salvation, bringing a sense of shared joy to all.

As the hymn progresses, it extends the invitation for creation itself to join in the jubilation. The imagery of fields, floods, rocks, hills, and plains rejoicing echoes the biblical idea of creation eagerly awaiting redemption. This visual description invites us to contemplate the cosmic significance of Christ's Advent and the transformative impact of His presence on the entire created order.

The hymn further emphasises the sovereign reign of Christ, affirming that He rules the world with truth and grace. This narrative element prompts reflection on the lordship of Christ in the lives of worshipers and the world at large. It encourages people to find comfort and assurance in the truth and grace that Christ brings.

The call to prepare hearts for the King also resonates with themes of spiritual readiness and devotion. It invites everyone to prepare a place for Christ in their lives and encourages introspection in the midst of the Christmas celebration.

The hymn concludes with a triumphant declaration of joy, reinforcing the enduring and contagious nature of the joy found in Christ. It serves as a call for us to share and spread the joy of salvation, embracing and extend the joyous message of his birth.

Morning Devotional

In the dawn of this new day, may I be inspired to spread joy to the world. In moments of challenge, may I carry a melody of joy and celebration, sharing the good news with those around me. Let the proclamation "And heaven and nature sing" be a constant reminder of the divine chorus that accompanies my steps, infusing each moment with the joyous spirit of Christ.

Evening Devotional

In the quiet of this evening and stillness of the night, may the message of celebration and the melodies of joy accompany my dreams. I open my heart to receive the King and prepare a space for His presence within me. As I rest, may the uplifting chorus of heaven and nature be a source of comfort and assurance, and a reminder that the celebration continues even in the quiet moments of the night.

14
O Christmas Tree

O Christmas Tree! O Christmas Tree!
Thy leaves are so unchanging;
O Christmas Tree! O Christmas Tree!
Thy leaves are so unchanging;
Not only green when summer's here,
But also when 'tis cold and drear.
O Christmas Tree! O Christmas Tree!
Thy leaves are so unchanging!

O Christmas Tree! O Christmas Tree!
Much pleasure thou can'st give me;
O Christmas Tree! O Christmas Tree!
Much pleasure thou can'st give me;
How often has the Christmas tree
Afforded me the greatest glee!
O Christmas Tree! O Christmas Tree!
Much pleasure thou can'st give me.

O Christmas Tree! O Christmas Tree!
Thy candles shine so brightly!
O Christmas Tree! O Christmas Tree!
Thy candles shine so brightly!
From base to summit, gay and bright,
There's only splendour for the sight.

O Christmas Tree! O Christmas Tree!
Thy candles shine so brightly!

O Christmas Tree! O Christmas Tree!
How richly God has decked thee!
O Christmas Tree! O Christmas Tree!
How richly God has decked thee!
Thou bidst us true and faithful be,
And trust in God unchangingly.
O Christmas Tree! O Christmas Tree!
How richly God has decked thee! !"

A brief history

"O Christmas Tree," or "O Tannenbaum" in its original German form, has roots deeply intertwined with German folk traditions. The melody of the carol is derived from a German folk song, and its lyrical transformation occurred in the early 20th century. Originally, the song praised the evergreen fir tree, a symbol of constancy and endurance. The lyrics extolled the tree's ability to retain its vibrant green foliage throughout the changing seasons, becoming a powerful symbol of steadfastness.

As the song evolved over time, it underwent a notable transformation into a Christmas carol. The transition from a general ode to the evergreen fir tree to a celebration of the Christmas tree marked a shift in the song's thematic focus. The Christmas tree, adorned with lights, ornaments, and festive decorations, became a central symbol of the holiday season.

The lyrics express admiration for the tree's branches that remain green both in summer and winter, emphasising the enduring vitality of the evergreen. The Christmas tree, with its unchanging foliage, came to symbolise not only constancy, but also the eternal beauty and renewal associated with the Christmas season.

The carol's popularity spread beyond Germany, becoming a cherished part of Christmas celebrations around the world. Its simple yet evocative lyrics and the familiar melody contribute to its enduring appeal. "O Christmas Tree" has become a classic in the repertoire of Christmas carols, embodying the festive spirit and symbolising the enduring traditions of the holiday season.

Through its journey from a folk song celebrating the steadfast evergreen to a beloved Christmas carol, "O Christmas Tree" continues to evoke the warmth and joy of the holiday season for people of various cultures and backgrounds.

Unwrapping the story

"O Christmas Tree," while not explicitly a religious hymn, has become a beloved part of the holiday season, often associated with the festive decor that adorns homes during Christmas and a reminder of the deeper spiritual themes woven into the Christmas celebration.

The hymn begins by celebrating the beauty and evergreen nature of the Christmas tree, also symbolising eternal life and pointing to the hope and promise of salvation found in Christ. This invites people to see beyond the external decorations to recognise the spiritual significance of the Christmas tree itself.

As the hymn progresses, it acknowledges the significance of the tree in winter, remaining green when other trees lose their leaves, representing the enduring hope and vitality that Christ brings, even during the metaphorical winters of life. People may find resonance in the idea that, through faith in Christ, they can remain spiritually vibrant in all seasons.

The hymn's focus on the Christmas tree as a symbol of fidelity and constancy, also introduces a narrative thread of steadfastness and the strength of faith. It offers inspiration for reflection, especially during the Christmas season when the birth of Christ exemplifies God's faithfulness to His promise of sending a Saviour

While not overtly theological, "O Christmas Tree" invites us to think about the spiritual symbolism of the Christmas tree, and to consider the deeper, eternal truths it represents.

Morning Prayer

With the morning light, let me turn my heart to the Christmas tree and see beyond the decorations to it's evergreen beauty and vitality. Help me find eternal hope in its constancy and resilience, and the promise of salvation through Christ. May my faith remain steadfast and vibrant through all seasons, trusting in Your unwavering faithfulness.

Evening Prayer

As night descends, let me turn my heart to the Christmas tree once more as a symbol of solace and calm. As I reflect on its evergreen branches may I find inspiration in Your devotion and constancy beyond the festivities. May its presence, adorned with memories and symbols of love and celebration, also become a sanctuary of peace. Let the twinkling lights illuminate my heart with gratitude for the day's moments of joy and connection, and reminder that Your love remains bright in my life.

15

O Come, All Ye Faithful

O Come All Ye Faithful
Joyful and triumphant,
O come ye, O come ye to Bethlehem.
Come and behold Him,
Born the King of Angels;

O come, let us adore Him,
O come, let us adore Him,
O come, let us adore Him,
Christ the Lord.

O Sing, choirs of angels,
Sing in exultation,
Sing all that hear in heaven God's holy word.
Give to our Father glory in the Highest;

O come, let us adore Him,
O come, let us adore Him,
O come, let us adore Him,
Christ the Lord.

All Hail! Lord, we greet Thee,
Born this happy morning,
O Jesus! for evermore be Thy name adored.
Word of the Father, now in flesh appearing;
O come, let us adore Him,
O come, let us adore Him,
O come, let us adore Him,
Christ the Lord.

A brief history

Carrying a rich history that spans centuries "O Come, All Ye Faithful," also known as "Adeste Fideles" in its Latin form, is attributed to John Francis Wade, an 18th-century Catholic layman. This hymn has evolved into an integral part of the Christmas musical tradition, resonating across generations and cultures.

The hymn's enduring popularity lies in its timeless call to the faithful, inviting them to journey to Bethlehem not only in the physical sense but, more profoundly, in heart and spirit. "O Come, All Ye Faithful" encapsulates the sheer joy and triumph associated with the Nativity, becoming a rallying cry for people to gather and adore the newborn King.

The hymn's lines resonate with the core Christian belief in the divinity of Christ, born of the virgin, bringing the Light of Light into the world. Through its stirring melody and reverent lyrics, the hymn has become a unifying force during the Christmas season, fostering a sense of communal worship and celebration.

As "O Come, All Ye Faithful" transcends linguistic boundaries, being sung in both Latin and various translations, its universal message of adoration and reverence continues to inspire countless individuals around the globe. The hymn serves as a musical embodiment of the Christmas spirit, calling worshipers to join together in praising the Christ child and celebrating the profound significance of His birth.

Unwrapping the story

"O Come, All Ye Faithful," is a familiar Christmas hymn, offering profound spiritual themes that resonate throughout Advent. Traditionally sung during the Christmas season, this hymn invites people to join in adoration and celebration of the birth of Jesus Christ.

The hymn opens with a joyous call to the faithful, urging them to come and behold the newborn King in Bethlehem. This sets the stage for a journey of worship and adoration, encouraging everyone to draw near to the Saviour with reverence and awe.

As the hymn progresses, it acknowledges the divine nature of the newborn King, describing Him as the "Word of the Father, now in flesh appearing." This narrative thread emphasises the Incarnation, where God takes on human form in the person of Jesus Christ. Serving as a poignant reminder of the extraordinary event that underlies the Christmas celebration.

The refrain, "O come, let us adore Him," becomes a powerful motif, echoing the call to worship and express deep reverence for the Christ child. People are invited to reflect on the adoration and devotion that should characterise their own worship, not just during the Christmas season but throughout the year.

The hymn's declaration of Jesus as the "Word of the Father" introduces an element that connects to the broader theological concept of Jesus as the embodiment of God's message and revelation to humanity. Readers may find in this an opportunity for contemplation on the significance of Christ's role in revealing God's love and truth.

In summary, "O Come, All Ye Faithful" becomes a lyrical story of worship, adoration, and contemplation for everyone. It takes us on a spiritual journey of reflection on the awe-inspiring mystery of the Incarnation, and inviting a deepened commitment to a life of faithful adoration of Jesus Christ.

Morning Devotion

As a new day unfolds may my heart draw near to the Saviour with reverence and awe. Let the call to the faithful at Christmas, the journey to Bethlehem, and the adoration of the newborn King resonate within. In the midst of daily tasks, let the refrain, "O come, let us adore Him," inspire and guide me inviting me to worship and express deep reverence for Christ.

Evening Devotion

As the day ends and I settle into the calm of the evening, let me recognise the faithfulness that has guided my thoughts and steps. May my adoration be a soothing balm bringing peace to my soul. In the stillness of night I recommit my heart to reverence and praise. As I lay down the concerns of this day, I seek your presence to calm my spirit and bring clarity to my thoughts.

16
O Holy Night

O holy night! The stars are brightly shining,
It is the night of the dear Saviour's birth.
Long lay the world in sin and error pining.
Till He appeared and the Spirit felt its worth.
A thrill of hope the weary world rejoices,
For yonder breaks a new and glorious morn.
Fall on your knees! Oh, hear the angel voices!
O night divine, the night when Christ was born;

O night, O holy night, O night divine!
O night, O holy night, O night divine!

Led by the light of faith serenely beaming,
With glowing hearts by His cradle we stand.
O'er the world a star is sweetly gleaming,
Now come the wisemen from out of the Orient land.
The King of kings lay thus lowly manger;
In all our trials born to be our friends.
He knows our need, our weakness is no stranger,

Behold your King! Before him lowly bend!
Behold your King! Before him lowly bend!

Truly He taught us to love one another,
His law is love and His gospel is peace.
Chains he shall break, for the slave is our brother.
And in his name all oppression shall cease.
Sweet hymns of joy in grateful chorus raise we,
With all our hearts we praise His holy name.
Christ is the Lord! Then ever, ever praise we,

His power and glory ever more proclaim!
His power and glory ever more proclaim!

A brief history

"O Holy Night," was originally written in French as "Minuit, chrétiens" by Placide Cappeau, a wine merchant and poet. With music composed by Adolphe Adam it offers a captivating narrative that resonates with the profound themes of the Christian faith. Commissioned for a Christmas Eve mass in 1847, the hymn quickly gained widespread popularity for its emotive lyrics and powerful melody.

As the hymn spread beyond its origins, it transcended linguistic boundaries, being translated into various languages. The universal themes of hope, redemption, and the transformative power of Christ's birth have contributed to its enduring appeal. "O Holy Night" stands as a testament to the ability of music and lyrics to evoke profound emotions and spiritual contemplation, inviting us all to reflect on the sacred beauty of the Christmas story.

Unwrapping the story

The hymn tells the story of the moment of Christ's birth, emphasising the stark contrast between the darkness of a world mired in sin and error, and the radiant hope brought by the Saviour's arrival. The lyrics paint a vivid picture of the night when Jesus was born, capturing the awe and joy felt by those who recognised the significance of the divine event. The palpable sense of wonder and reverence conveyed through the verses and music has resonated deeply with audiences, making "O Holy Night" a cherished and emotional piece in the Christmas musical repertoire.

The hymn unfolds as a poignant narrative that commences with a peaceful setting on the night of Christ's birth, portraying a serene atmosphere contrasting with the profound implications of the event. This tranquil scene becomes the backdrop for the powerful story of the arrival of the Saviour, inviting us to envision the holy night when Jesus entered the world.

The central message revolves around the realisation of a long-awaited promise - the arrival of a Redeemer who would bring salvation to humanity. The hymn beautifully describes the moment when Christ's birth was announced, capturing the anticipation and significance of the event. This invites people to reflect on the divine fulfilment of prophecies and the profound impact of Christ's birth on the course of human history.

As the hymn progresses it shifts to a more personal tone, with the words expressing gratitude for the redemptive message of Christmas. The refrain, "Fall on your knees, O hear the angel voices," becomes a climactic moment, urging everyone to respond with humility, reverence, and a sense of awe. We are invited to experience the transformative power of encountering the Saviour and responding with a heart full of adoration. It encourages a personal response of humility, worship, and gratitude for the redemptive message heralded on that holy night.

Morning Prayer

As I embark on this new day, I am mindful of the opportunities it holds for growth and compassion. In the simplicity of daily routines, may moments of joy and gratitude. Help me to recognise the sacredness in the ordinary, just as the world paused in awe on that holy night. In the midst of the seasonal rush, guide me to appreciate life's simple pleasures and share kindness with those I encounter. May my heart join in the heavenly chorus, not just during this Christmas season, but in every season.

Evening Prayer

As the day draws to a close, I reflect on the moments that unfolded. In the quiet of the night, I seek your presence. Just as the shepherds marvelled at the celestial spectacle, let me marvel at the blessings and lessons of this day. As I lay down to rest, I surrender the concerns of the day, finding comfort in your love. Let the peace of that holy night fill my heart, and may the angels' joy be the lullaby that accompanies my sleep. In this season of reflection and anticipation, I offer my prayers, grateful for the gift of each day and the promise of new beginnings.

17
O Little Town of Bethlehem

O little town of Bethlehem
How still we see thee lie
Above thy deep and dreamless sleep
The silent stars go by
Yet in thy dark streets shineth
The everlasting Light
The hopes and fears of all the years
Are met in thee tonight

For Christ is born of Mary
And gathered all above
While mortals sleep, the angels keep
Their watch of wondering love
O morning stars together
Proclaim the holy birth
And praises sing to God the King
And Peace to men on earth

How silently, how silently
The wondrous gift is given!
So God imparts to human hearts
The blessings of His heaven.
No ear may his His coming,
But in this world of sin,

Where meek souls will receive him still,
The dear Christ enters in.

O holy Child of Bethlehem
Descend to us, we pray
Cast out our sin and enter in
Be born to us today
We hear the Christmas angels
The great glad tidings tell
O come to us, abide with us
Our Lord Emmanuel.

A brief history

"O Little Town of Bethlehem" is a Christmas carol with lyrics written by Phillips Brooks, an Episcopal priest, and music composed by Lewis Redner, a church organist. The hymn originated in the context of a journey that Brooks took to the Holy Land in 1865. During his visit, he was struck by the serene and peaceful atmosphere of Bethlehem, especially the starlit night. Inspired by his experiences, Brooks penned the lyrics to "O Little Town of Bethlehem" three years later in 1868.

Upon returning to the United States, Brooks shared the lyrics with Redner, the organist at his church, who then composed the music. The hymn was first performed during the Christmas season at Brooks' church, the Holy Trinity Church in Philadelphia, in 1868. Over the years, "O Little Town of Bethlehem" gained widespread popularity and became a familiar part of Christmas celebrations around the world.

The hymn captures the essence of the Christmas story, inviting everyone to contemplate the humble birth of Jesus in Bethlehem. Its enduring appeal lies in its ability to convey the universal themes of peace and goodwill associated with the Nativity.

Unwrapping the story

"O Little Town of Bethlehem" paints a vivid picture of the humble yet significant setting of the birth of Jesus Christ. This beloved Christmas hymn invites us to step into the serene town of Bethlehem on that sacred night, and contemplate the profound themes of peace, hope, and divine intervention.

The hymn begins by setting the scene, describing the quiet and stillness that envelop the town under the starry sky. The story then shifts to the profound significance of Bethlehem, chosen as the birthplace of the Saviour according to ancient prophecies. Readers are drawn into the historical narrative, reflecting on the divine orchestration behind the events leading to the birth of Jesus.

A central theme of the hymn revolves around the paradoxical nature of Christ's arrival - a humble, unassuming birth with monumental implications for humanity. The story highlights the contrast between ordinary and extraordinary, focusing on the divine unfolding in a small town.

The second verse introduces the concept of Christ's love binding people together, transcending earthly divisions. The hymn encourages everyone to reflect on the universal impact of Christ's birth, fostering unity and brotherhood among people of all backgrounds.

The final verse of the hymn presents a call to listeners to receive Christ into their hearts, echoing the biblical invitation for us all to welcome the Saviour. The lyrical arc of the hymn, from the quiet streets of Bethlehem to the universal message of Christ's love, creates a profound sense of connection between the historical event and people's ongoing spiritual journey.

In essence, "O Little Town of Bethlehem" offers a narrative that transports us to the heart of the Christmas story, prompting reflection on the miraculous events and the enduring impact of Christ's birth. The hymn encourages us to embrace the message of hope, peace, and divine love as we contemplate the significance of Bethlehem in the glory of God's redemptive plan.

Morning Devotional

As I begin this new day I reflect on the serenity of Bethlehem, illuminated by the star that guided the way to the birthplace of Christ. May I carry the peace of that sacred night in my heart, recognising the divine presence in the ordinary moments of life. Like the shepherds who witnessed the extraordinary, let me hear the whispers of hope and joy as I go about my daily routines. As I navigate through this day, may the universal message of peace and goodwill inspire my actions, fostering unity and love.

Evening Devotional

As the day ends I turn my thoughts to the arrival of the Saviour, and the tranquility that comes from your divine presence. In the stillness of this night may hope and love guide my reflections. As I rest, I surrender the concerns of the day, finding solace in the eternal holy story. In this season of contemplation, I offer my prayers, grateful for the enduring message of hope and the promise of divine love.

18
Once in Royal David's City

Once in royal Davids city,
Stood a lowly cattle shed,
Where a mother laid her Baby,
In a manger for His bed:
Mary was that mother mild,
Jesus Christ, her little Child.

He came down to earth from heaven,
Who is God and Lord of all,
And His shelter was a stable,
And His cradle was a stall:
With the poor, and mean, and lowly,
Lived on earth our Saviour holy.

For He is our childhood's pattern;
Day by day, like us, He grew;
He was little, weak, and helpless,
Tears and smiles, like us He knew;
And He cares when we are sad,
And he shares when we are glad.

And our eyes at last shall see Him,
Through His own redeeming love;
For that Child so dear and gentle,
Is our Lord in heaven above:
And He leads His children on,
To the place where He is gone.

A brief history

"Once in Royal David's City" stands as a testament to the creative genius of Cecil Frances Alexander, an esteemed Irish hymn writer and poet of the 19th century. Born in 1818, Alexander's contributions to Christian hymnody and her dedication to religious education, particularly for children, have left an indelible mark on the world of sacred music.

Composed during the Victorian era, the hymn emerged as part of a larger movement to bring hymnody into the realm of everyday life and foster a deeper connection between religious teachings and the broader community. Cecil Frances Alexander's hymns, characterised by their lyrical beauty and theological depth, played a crucial role in achieving this goal.

The hymn itself was penned as a reflection on the Nativity story, capturing the essence of the humble birth of Jesus in Bethlehem. The hymn's first appearance was in Mrs. Alexander's collection titled "Hymns for Little Children," published in 1848. The simplicity and poignancy of the lyrics, combined with a captivating melody, contributed to the hymn's rapid acceptance and its enduring place in the Christmas musical repertoire.

Unwrapping the story

"Once in Royal David's City" transports us to the heart Christmas, exploring the themes of humility, redemption, and the divine purpose of the birth of Christ. Its opening lines transport listeners to Bethlehem, the quiet, historical town where, in a lowly stable, a miraculous event unfolds. The lyrics vividly depict the scene, portraying Mary, the Virgin, cradling her newborn son, Jesus, in a humble manger. The use of evocative imagery captures the simplicity and humility of the Nativity, emphasising the unexpected setting for the arrival of the King of kings.

Beyond recounting this momentous event, the hymn delves into profound theological themes. It reflects on the divine mystery of the Incarnation - the belief that God took on human form in the person of Jesus Christ. The hymn emphasises the paradoxical nature of this act, where the majestic and eternal King chooses to enter the world in the most unassuming and vulnerable manner. The hymn prompts us to reflect on the profound contrast between the grandeur often associated with royalty and the unassuming nature of Christ's birth.

As the hymn progresses, it traces the life of Jesus, highlighting key moments from His childhood to His ministry. The narrative captures the essence of Christ's earthly journey, emphasising His humanity and the challenges He faced. A pivotal moment in the hymn is the call to follow in Christ's footsteps - to be gentle and lowly in spirit, mirroring the humility displayed in the Saviour's life. We are all prompted to contemplate the transformative power of Christ's teachings and the redemptive purpose behind His sacrificial death on the cross.

Morning Reflection

As I find myself embraced by a new day I picture the simplicity and humility of the place that Jesus came into the world. As I navigate the day ahead, help me to find beauty in unexpected moments and recognise Your presence in the ordinary. Guide me to be gentle and lowly in spirit, and may my day unfold with moments of kindness, understanding, and grace.

Evening Reflection

As the evening descends and the day begins to slow I turn my heart to reflect on the image of a humble manger where Jesus Christ was born. May I recognise moments of joy, hope, and transformation for myself and others. As I rest, may humility and redemption shape my dreams, reminding me of the divine purpose behind Christ's arrival. In this season of contemplation, I offer my prayers, grateful for the enduring message of hope and the transformative power of Your love.

19
Silent Night

Silent night, holy night
All is calm, all is bright
Round yon Virgin Mother and Child
Holy Infant so tender and mild

Sleep in heavenly peace
Sleep in heavenly peace

Silent night, holy night!
Shepherds quake at the sight
Glories stream from heaven afar
Heavenly hosts sing Alleluia!

Christ, the Saviour is born
Christ, the Saviour is born

Silent night, holy night
Son of God, love's pure light
Radiant beams from Thy holy face
With the dawn of redeeming grace

Jesus, Lord, at Thy birth
Jesus, Lord, at Thy birth

A brief history

"Silent Night," also known as "Stille Nacht" in its original German, remains a masterpiece amongst Christmas carols. It was composed by Joseph Mohr, a young Austrian priest, and set to music by Franz Xaver Gruber, a schoolteacher. The genesis of this iconic hymn lies in the quaint town of Oberndorf, Austria, during the early 19th century. Legend intertwines with history as it narrates that the church's organ in Oberndorf was broken, prompting the creation of this simple yet profound hymn, accompanied by the gentle strumming of a guitar.

The hymn unfolds as a story of the serene and miraculous atmosphere of the first Christmas night. "Silent Night" delicately weaves a tale of the quiet and peace that enveloped the birth of Jesus in Bethlehem. It paints a vivid picture of shepherds, guided by heavenly hosts, bearing witness to the Redeemer's arrival in a humble manger. The tender lullaby becomes a poignant expression of the awe and reverence inspired by the sight of the Holy Infant.

Beyond the historical circumstances of its creation, "Silent Night" has become a global phenomenon, transcending linguistic boundaries and cultural divides. In recognition of its cultural importance, UNESCO declared "Silent Night" as an intangible cultural heritage in 2011. Its simple yet profound lyrics and melody evoke the universal emotions of wonder, tranquility, and adoration associated with the Nativity. As the hymn continues to echo through countless Christmas celebrations, it remains a testament to the enduring power of music to convey the timeless story of the Holy Night.

Unwrapping the story

"Silent Night" draws people straight into the serene and sacred atmosphere surrounding the birth of Jesus, Opening with a tranquil scene - the world enveloped in stillness on that holy night in Bethlehem. The quietude becomes a canvas for the profound events that unfold and the arrival of the long-awaited Messiah.

The hymn beautifully describes the scene of Mary cradling the infant Jesus in the peaceful setting of a stable. It underscores the intimacy and simplicity of the moment, inviting us to contemplate the divine significance of this humble birth. As the hymn progresses, the narrative introduces the shepherds who, guided by the light of the star, witness the miraculous birth. This segment of the hymn emphasises the universality of the message - how the good news of Christ's birth is shared not with the powerful or privileged but with those living on the margins of society.

The story deepens as the hymn introduces the concept of heavenly peace, a gift brought by the Christ child. Listeners are prompted to reflect on the transformative power of God's love, symbolised by the arrival of Jesus, and to embrace the hope and peace that His presence brings.

"Silent Night" concludes with a universal call to praise and worship, echoing the angelic chorus heard by the shepherds. The hymn's narrative arc guides readers through the stillness of that sacred night, inviting them to experience the awe, wonder, and profound peace emanating from the birth of the Saviour It serves as a timeless reminder of the divine significance of Christmas and the eternal peace offered through the Christ child.

Morning Devotional

As the day begins I take a moment to centre myself in the midst of the daily hustle. In the quiet of this morning may the simplicity and wonder of that sacred night infuse my day with a sense of peace. As I step into the challenges ahead, may the echoes of "Silent Night" guide my interactions, reminding me to approach each moment with awe and kindness.

Evening Devotional

As the day comes to a close I pause to unwind and reflect. In the stillness of this evening, just as that night in Bethlehem brought tranquility, may peace settle my mind. In the quiet moments before sleep I release the stresses of the day. May I be grateful for the wisdom of the Christmas story and carry its comforting presence into the night, ready to embrace a new day tomorrow.

20
The First Noel

The First Noel, the Angels did say
Was to certain poor shepherds in fields as they lay
In fields where they lay keeping their sheep
On a cold winter's night that was so deep.
Noel, Noel, Noel, Noel
Born is the King of Israel!

They looked up and saw a star
Shining in the East beyond them far
And to the earth it gave great light
And so it continued both day and night.
Noel, Noel, Noel, Noel
Born is the King of Israel!

And by the light of that same star
Three Wise men came from country far
To seek for a King was their intent
And to follow the star wherever it went.
Noel, Noel, Noel, Noel
Born is the King of Israel!

This star drew nigh to the northwest
O'er Bethlehem it took its rest
And there it did both Pause and stay
Right o'er the place where Jesus lay.
Noel, Noel, Noel, Noel
Born is the King of Israel!

Then entered in those Wise men three
Full reverently upon their knee
And offered there in His presence
Their gold and myrrh and frankincense.
Noel, Noel, Noel, Noel
Born is the King of Israel!

Then let us all with one accord
Sing praises to our heavenly Lord
That hath made Heaven and earth of nought
And with his blood mankind has bought.
Noel, Noel, Noel, Noel
Born is the King of Israel!

A brief history

"The First Noel" is believed to have originated in the 16th or 17th century. The term "Noel" is derived from the French word "nouvelles," meaning news or tidings, underscoring the hymn's role as a bearer of joyful announcements.

The creators of the hymn, both writer and composer, remain unknown, a common feature of traditional carols with origins steeped in the collective spirit of their times. Despite this mystery, "The First Noel" has endured over the centuries, becoming a significant part of the Christmas musical celebrations. The hymn recounts the angelic message to shepherds and the Wise Men's journey guided by a celestial star, encapsulating the essence of the Christmas story. Its longevity speaks to its universal appeal, making it a cherished melody that resonates through time, inviting each listener to connect with the ageless journey to Bethlehem.

Unwrapping the story

"The First Noel" weaves a narrative that invites people to immerse themselves in the moment of Jesus' birth. It opens with the announcement of the angelic proclamation to shepherds tending their flocks under the starry night. This celestial announcement marks the beginning of a divine story that will forever change the course of history.

Through its lyrics the hymn beautifully captures the sense of anticipation and wonder as the shepherds gaze upon the radiant star, appointed to guide them to the newborn King. The refrain repeated at the end of each verse throughout the carol serves as a melodic reminder of the joyous nature of this momentous occasion.

As the hymn progresses, the story expands to include the visitation of the wise men, guided by the same celestial light. This convergence of humble shepherds and esteemed Magi underscores the universality of Christ's birth, bringing together individuals from all walks of life to witness the fulfilment of ancient prophecies.

The hymn reaches its peak with the adoration of the newborn King. Contrasting shepherds and the wise men emphasises the inclusivity of God's redemptive plan, inviting people to reflect on the significance of Jesus' birth for both the lowly and the learned.

A triumphant proclamation of praise to celebrate the grandeur of the event concludes the carol where everyone is invited to join the heavenly chorus in exalting the newborn King.

Morning Prayer

In the quiet dawn, I open my heart to the messages You might bring into my life today. In the midst of tasks and responsibilities, I seek the radiant light of Christ. Like the wise men, I aspire to be drawn toward Your presence, letting the guiding star of Your grace illuminate my path. Whether in moments of reflection or bustling activity help me share kindness and joy with those I encounter.

Evening Prayer

In the quietude of this evening, I reflect on the day's journey, humbly presenting the gifts of my heart in Your presence. May my actions and intentions be offerings of love, reverence, and devotion. As I close my eyes, let me see the starry night serving as a reminder of Your constant presence. In the stillness, grant me peaceful rest and gratitude, knowing that I am cradled in Your love.

21
The Holly and the Ivy

The holly and the ivy,
When they are both full grown;
Of all the trees that are in the wood
The holly bears the crown.
O the rising of the sun,
And the running of the deer,
The playing of the merry organ
Sweet singing of the choir.

The holly bears a blossom,
As white as lily flower;
And Mary bore sweet Jesus Christ
To be our sweet Saviour.
O the rising of the sun,
And the running of the deer,
The playing of the merry organ
Sweet singing of the choir.

The holly bears a berry,
As red as any blood;
And Mary bore sweet Jesus Christ
To do poor sinners good.
O the rising of the sun,
And the running of the deer,

The playing of the merry organ
Sweet singing of the choir.

The holly bears a prickle,
As sharp as any thorn;
And Mary bore sweet Jesus Christ
On Christmas Day in the morn.
O the rising of the sun,
And the running of the deer,
The playing of the merry organ
Sweet singing of the choir.

The holly bears a bark,
As bitter as any gall;
And Mary bore sweet Jesus Christ
For to redeem us all.
O the rising of the sun,
And the running of the deer,
The playing of the merry organ
Sweet singing of the choir.

The holly and the ivy,
Now both are full well grown;
Of all the trees that are in the wood
The holly bears the crown.
O the rising of the sun,
And the running of the deer,
The playing of the merry organ
Sweet singing of the choir.

A brief history

"The Holly and the Ivy" is an English carol with roots reaching back to the 18th century. The carol's enduring popularity lies in its light and joyful melody and unique blend of pagan symbolism with Christmas themes. While its precise origin remains somewhat elusive, it is believed to have originated in rural England where communities celebrated the Christmas season with a blend of Christian and pre-Christian customs.

The melody and composition of this delightful carols adds another layer to its historical significance. Although the original composer remains unknown, the carol's tunes have evolved over time, adapting to various arrangements and interpretations. This adaptability has contributed to the hymn's widespread popularity and enduring presence in Christmas celebrations.

Through its rich history, intricate symbolism, and melodic variations, "The Holly and the Ivy" has become a delightful part of the Christmas musical canon. Its ability to bridge the natural world with Christian theology offers people a unique and captivating perspective on the timeless themes of Christmas, making it a perennial favourite during the holiday
season.

Unwrapping the story

"The Holly and the Ivy" encapsulates the rich symbolism of Christmas traditions inviting people to explore the profound meanings behind familiar holiday elements. The hymn starts with the juxtaposition of the holly and the ivy, two symbolic plants deeply rooted in Christmas lore.

The carol's lyrics intertwine the natural imagery of holly and ivy with profound Christian symbolism. Holly, personifying Jesus Christ, is depicted through its prickly leaves, which draw a poignant parallel to the crown of thorns worn during the crucifixion. The red berries symbolise the drops of blood shed for humanity's redemption, and the crown represents the kingly stature of Christ. In contrast, the ivy, symbolising humanity, is woven into the through the story to represent unity and the interconnectedness between people and the divine.

As the verses unfold, the holly representing the Nativity and Christ's sacrifice is contrasted, the ivy, and its evergreen nature, signifying enduring life and the promise of eternal salvation. This interplay of symbols creates a visual story, encouraging people to reflect on the dual nature of Christ's birth - the earthly and the divine.

The story progresses to the gathering of the holly and the ivy as a communal celebration where people come together to honour the birth of Christ. This festive gathering is a metaphorical tableau of unity, reminding us of the universal significance of Christmas.

The hymn delicately introduces the Virgin Mary and the baby Jesus through the the Nativity scene. The ivy's mention of "shepherdess and shepherd" emphasises the inclusivity of the Christmas story, extending an invitation to all to be welcomed into this joyous occasion. The final verses exalt the triumphant reign of Christ, with the hymn, like the intertwining vines, bringing together the earthly and the divine in a joint celebration.

Morning Reflection

In the quiet dawn, I reflect on the intertwining themes of holly and ivy. Let the prickly leaves of holly remind me of sacrifice and redemption, acting as a call to live with purpose and kindness. As I navigate the day, may I carry the spirit of unity symbolised by the ivy, embracing connections with others and recognizing the divine in our shared humanity.

Evening Reflection

As the day comes to an end I meditate on the Nativity scene depicted by the holly and the ivy. Just as they intertwine in harmony, may my life be woven with compassion, understanding, and unity. In this moment of reflection, I appreciate the interconnectedness of all, celebrating the universal significance of shared joy and hope.

22
The Twelve Days of Christmas (1909)

On the first day of Christmas,
my true love sent to me
A Partridge in a Pear Tree.

On the second day of Christmas,
my true love sent to me
Two Turtle Doves
And a Partridge in a Pear Tree.

On the third day of Christmas,
my true love sent to me
Three French Hens,
Two Turtle Doves,
And a Partridge in a Pear Tree.

On the fourth day of Christmas,
my true love sent to me
Four Calling Birds,
Three French Hens,
Two Turtle Doves,
And a Partridge in a Pear Tree.

On the fifth day of Christmas,
my true love sent to me
Five Gold Rings.
Four Calling Birds,
Three French Hens,
Two Turtle Doves,
And a Partridge in a Pear Tree.

A brief history

The Twelve Days of Christmas traditionally refer to the period between Christmas Day, December 25th, and the Feast of the Epiphany, which falls on January 6th. These days are considered a festive season in many Christian traditions.

The origin of the Twelve Days of Christmas can be traced back to medieval and Tudor England, where the period was marked by various celebrations, feasts, and revelry. The culmination of the Twelve Days is the Feast of the Epiphany, which commemorates the visit of the Magi, or the Three Wise Men, to the infant Jesus. This event symbolises the revelation of Jesus to the Gentiles.

In some cultures, especially in Western Christianity, each day of the Twelve Days is associated with a particular saint or religious figure, adding a layer of religious observance to the festive season. Over time, various customs and traditions have developed around the Twelve Days of Christmas, including the popular Christmas carol "The Twelve Days of Christmas," which playfully enumerates gifts given each day.

This carol has origins deeply rooted in English tradition, believed to have emerged during the 18th century. Beyond its musical charm, the song was originally associated with a memory-and-forfeit game, adding an interactive and playful dimension to its history. The game's structure involved participants taking turns reciting verses of the song, with each verse adding a new element to the cumulative list of gifts. The game's loser, at the end of reciting all the accumulated gifts, had to perform a task or present a small gift. This element added a lively and participatory aspect to the celebration of the Twelve Days of Christmas.

The lyrics of the song paint a vivid picture of a series of extravagant and whimsical gifts bestowed by a true love over the twelve days of the Christmas season. From a partridge in a pear tree to twelve drummers drumming, each verse contributes to the growing list of presents, creating a delightful and imaginative narrative.

The precise origins of the melody and composer are a bit elusive, with the carol evolving over time and being passed down through generations. The song's enduring popularity and playful tone have contributed to its continued presence in Christmas celebrations worldwide, with various adaptations and interpretations reflecting the festive and joyful spirit of the season.

While modern celebrations often focus primarily on Christmas Day, understanding the historical significance of the Twelve Days of Christmas helps us appreciate the rich traditions that contribute to the Christmas season.

Unwrapping the story

"The Twelve Days of Christmas" is a clever visual narrative that captures the essence of a unique Christmas celebration. With its cumulative structure, this enduring carol introduces us to a series of delightful gifts exchanged over twelve days.

The hymn begins with the grand bestowal of a "partridge in a pear tree." The singular nature of this gift sets the stage for a cascade of presents, each building on the previous day's offerings. The carol takes us on a rich and festive journey, revealing the extravagant and sometimes eccentric gifts lavished upon the recipient.
As the days progress, the cumulative effect creates a sense of abundance and jubilation. The rhythmic repetition of each gift contributes to the seasonal atmosphere, inviting people to envision the lively and generous spirit of Christmas .

Amid the whimsy, the carol subtly incorporates Christian symbolism. The partridge, often associated with sacrifice, serves as a metaphor for Christ's selfless love. The subsequent gifts, ranging from turtle doves to lords-a-leaping, contribute to a celebration that echoes the joyous proclamation of Christ's birth. The carol ends with all the gifts recited together transforming the song into a jolly shared chorus, fostering a sense of community and joint merriment.

Morning Prayer

As I journey through the twelve days of Christmas, may I embrace the communal spirit of giving and celebration. Like the gifts in the carol, may each day bring moments of abundance and jubilation. Let the rhythm of joy fill my heart, and may I share in the merriment that echoes the joyous proclamation of Christ's birth.

Evening Prayer

As I read the end of another day, I reflect on the unique gifts Christmas brings us. May each day bring its own blessings, and the cumulative effect of every day be a reminder of the abundance of love and joy found in Jesus Christ and his birth.

23
The Wassail Song

Here we come a-wassailing
Among the leaves so green,
Here we come a-wand'ring
So fair to be seen.
Love and joy come to you,
And to you your wassail, too,
And God bless you, and send you
A Happy New Year,
And God send you a Happy New Year.

We are not daily beggars
That beg from door to door,
But we are neighbours' children
Whom you have seen before
Love and joy come to you,
And to you your wassail, too,
And God bless you, and send you
A Happy New Year,
And God send you a Happy New Year.

Good master and good mistress,
As you sit beside the fire,
Pray think of us poor children
Who wander in the mire.

Love and joy come to you,
And to you your wassail, too,
And God bless you, and send you
A Happy New Year,
And God send you a Happy New Year

We have a little purse
Made of ratching leather skin;
We want some of your small change
To line it well within.
Love and joy come to you,
And to you your wassail, too,
And God bless you, and send you
A Happy New Year,
And God send you a Happy New Year.

Bring us out a table
And spread it with a cloth;
Bring us out a cheese,
And of your Christmas loaf.
Love and joy come to you,
And to you your wassail, too,
And God bless you, and send you
A Happy New Year,
And God send you a Happy New Year.

God bless the master of this house,
Likewise the mistress too;
And all the little children
That round the table go.
Love and joy come to you,
And to you your wassail, too,
And God bless you, and send you

A Happy New Year,
And God send you a Happy New Year.

Here we come a-wassailing
Among the leaves so green,
Here we come a-wand'ring
So fair to be seen.
Love and joy come to you,
And to you your wassail, too,
And God bless you, and send you
A Happy New Year,
And God send you a Happy New Year.

We are not daily beggars
That beg from door to door,
But we are neighbours' children
Whom you have seen before
Love and joy come to you,
And to you your wassail, too,
And God bless you, and send you
A Happy New Year,
And God send you a Happy New Year.

Good master and good mistress,
As you sit beside the fire,
Pray think of us poor children
Who wander in the mire.
Love and joy come to you,
And to you your wassail, too,
And God bless you, and send you
A Happy New Year,
And God send you a Happy New Year

We have a little purse
Made of ratching leather skin;
We want some of your small change
To line it well within.
Love and joy come to you,
And to you your wassail, too,
And God bless you, and send you
A Happy New Year,
And God send you a Happy New Year.

Bring us out a table
And spread it with a cloth;
Bring us out a cheese,
And of your Christmas loaf.
Love and joy come to you,
And to you your wassail, too,
And God bless you, and send you
A Happy New Year,
And God send you a Happy New Year.

God bless the master of this house,
Likewise the mistress too;
And all the little children
That round the table go.
Love and joy come to you,
And to you your wassail, too,
And God bless you, and send you
A Happy New Year,
And God send you a Happy New Year.

A brief history

Deeply rooted in English folklore "The Wassail Song" is a traditional carol associated with the historial custom of wassailing, a medieval drinking ritual performed during the Christmas season. The term "wassail" itself comes from the Old Norse phrase "ves heill," meaning "be in good health" or "be fortunate."

The carol's origins can be traced back to the medieval period, with its lyrics evolving over time. Wassailing was a communal tradition where people would gather to sing and celebrate, often going door-to-door to wish their neighbours well and share in the festive spirit. The lyrics of the Wassail Song reflect the joyous and convivial nature of this practice.

The specific origins of the song's composition are less clear, as it was likely passed down through generations in an oral tradition. The melody and lyrics were shaped by various communities over time, contributing to the song's regional variations.

The themes of this song are centred around good wishes, abundance, and communal merriment. The singers express a desire for health and prosperity for those they visit, invoking blessings upon the household and its occupants. The act of wassailing itself was often accompanied by the sharing of a spiced ale or mulled cider, symbolising hospitality and good cheer.

Overall, the Wassail Song stands as a testament to the rich tapestry of Christmas traditions, blending festive music, well-wishing, and communal celebrations that have endured through the centuries.

Unwrapping the story

"The Wassail Song" invites everyone to join in a spirited celebration, capturing the essence of a centuries-old tradition with its lively and festive narrative. This carol, rooted in the custom of wassailing - an ancient English practice of toasting to health and prosperity- immerses everyone in the warmth and conviviality of a winter gathering.

The hymn unfolds as a jovial invitation to join in the revelry, encouraging all to partake in the festivities. The term "wassail" itself is a wish for good health, underscoring the carol's emphasis on joint well-being and shared merriment.

Throughout the verses, the carol paints a vivid picture of a happy celebration. From the orchards to the streets, the wassailers spread good cheer and abundance, creating a sense of camaraderie and shared blessings. The rhythmic repetition of the chorus enhances the sense of festivity, inviting people to imagine the lively atmosphere of the wassailing tradition.

Beyond the surface revelry, the carol also captures the Christian spirit of the season. The act of wishing health and joy aligns with the message of love and goodwill associated with Christmas. We are encouraged to see the wassailing tradition as a reflection of the broader Christmas narrative, a time of coming together, sharing blessings, and expressing gratitude for the gift of life.

As the Wassail Song concludes, it leaves readers with a lingering sense of warmth and conviviality, encouraging everyone to embrace the festive spirit and extend goodwill to others during the season of Advent. We are all invited to view the carol as a joyful celebration of community, shared blessings, and the timeless message of Christ's love.

Morning Prayer

With the sun's arrival, I embrace the spirit of wassailing, recognising the importance of shared joy in our shared lives. As I step into this new day, may my actions be infused with love, warmth and togetherness. May I bless the endeavours of each person I encounter, offering encouragement and support. Let me be reminded of the power found in shared moments, and may this collective joy be a source of strength for the challenges ahead.

Evening Prayer

As evening descends I carry the blessings and joy of this day in my reflections. Let gratitude fill my soul as I look back on the shared moments of the day. In the quiet of the night my prayers extend wishes of peace, joy, and prosperity to all. May the echoes of communal celebration be shared, and in the stillness, may I find solace and connection, knowing that the power of shared joy transcends the passing of the day.

24
We Three Kings

We three kings of Orient are
Bearing gifts we traverse afar
Field and fountain, moor and mountain
Following yonder star

O Star of wonder, star of night
Star with royal beauty bright
Westward leading, still proceeding
Guide us to thy Perfect Light

Born a King on Bethlehem's plain
Gold I bring to crown Him again
King forever, ceasing never
Over us all to rein

O Star of wonder, star of night
Star with royal beauty bright
Westward leading, still proceeding
Guide us to Thy perfect light

Frankincense to offer have I
Incense owns a Deity nigh
Pray'r and praising, all men raising
Worship Him, God most high

O Star of wonder, star of night
Star with royal beauty bright
Westward leading, still proceeding
Guide us to Thy perfect light

Myrrh is mine, its bitter perfume
Breathes of life of gathering gloom
Sorrowing, sighing, bleeding, dying
Sealed in the stone-cold tomb

O Star of wonder, star of night
Star with royal beauty bright
Westward leading, still proceeding
Guide us to Thy perfect light

Glorious now behold Him arise
King and God and Sacrifice
Alleluia, Alleluia
Earth to heav'n replies

O Star of wonder, star of night
Star with royal beauty bright
Westward leading, still proceeding
Guide us to Thy perfect light .

A brief history

"We Three Kings," penned by John Henry Hopkins Jr. in 1857, holds a unique place in the Christmas hymn repertoire. John Hopkins, an Episcopal clergyman, composed this hymn with a specific purpose in mind: to enhance a Christmas pageant at the General Theological Seminary in New York City.

The lyrics tell the story of the journey of the Magi, or Wise Men, who traveled from the East who undertook a remarkable journey from the East honour the newborn King, Jesus. Each of the three kings carries a profound and symbolic gift - gold, representing the recognition of Jesus as a king; frankincense, symbolising the acknowledgment of His divine nature; and myrrh, a poignant foreshadowing of the sacrifice and death that would mark His redemptive mission.

Rooted in the Gospel of Matthew this story becomes a focal point of the hymn. Hopkins employs vivid imagery to capture the essence of the Magi's expedition, their reverence for the Christ child, and the symbolic significance of the gifts they bring. In this way, "We Three Kings" serves as both a historical reflection on the Magi's journey and a poignant reminder of the profound spiritual significance of the gifts they presented at the Nativity scene.

The hymn's enduring appeal lies not only in its historical context but also in its ability to transport listeners to the heart of this event. The melody, composed by Hopkins himself, adds a layer of emotional resonance to the lyrical narrative. Over the years, "We Three Kings" has become a cherished part of Christmas traditions, reminding believers of the profound journey made by the Wise Men to witness the birth of Jesus.

Unwrapping the story

"We Three Kings" takes us on a majestic journey that evokes the awe and wonder of the Magi's expedition to witness the birth of Jesus. With its stately melody the carol brings to life the story of the wise men, their pilgrimage, and the profound significance of the gifts they bring.

It begins by introducing us to the three kings, each representing a different region and cultural background. Following the Star of Bethlehem, we join the Magi in their quest, traversing vast deserts and rugged terrains, guided solely by the celestial light.

The verses unfold like a poetic travelogue, describing the symbolic significance of the gifts- gold, frankincense, and myrrh. These offerings, in addition to their material value, hold deep spiritual meaning, foreshadowing Jesus' identity as a king, priest, and sacrifice.

As the carol progresses the atmosphere grows more contemplative, prompting singers and listeners to reflect on the theological implications of the journey. The overarching theme becomes an exploration of faith and the recognition of the divine in the humblest of settings.

The carol's chorus, with its melodic repetition of "Star of wonder, star of night," captures the essence of the Magi's awe and adoration. It invites people to join in the contemplative spirit of the journey, encouraging us to recognise the divine light guiding our own paths.

In essence, "We Three Kings" tells the biblical story of the Magi's pilgrimage through carefully crafted words and music, inviting everyone to share in the wonder, humility, and reverence that defined that sacred journey. As a devotional, Christian readers can find inspiration in the carol's exploration of faith, the symbolic gifts, and the acknowledgment of Christ's divine presence.

Morning Devotional

In the stillness of this morning, may this day unfold as a pilgrimage, filled with opportunities to offer the gifts of love, compassion, and grace. As I navigate my daily life, let light guide my steps. In moments of decision and choice, may the symbolism of the gifts inspire me to offer the treasures of my heart. Just as the Magi followed the Star of Bethlehem, may I follow the guiding light in my own journey, trusting that it will lead me to moments of awe and revelation.

Evening Devotional

As the days ends I think about the symbolic gifts of gold, frankincense, and myrrh presented by the Wise Men. Let me reflect on the profound meanings embedded in each offering. May I, too, bring the treasures of my heart, acknowledgment, reverence, and sacrifice, to the places in my life where they are needed. May my gifts be symbols of love and devotion, aligning with the spiritual significance revealed through these offerings.

25
While Shepherds Watched Their Flocks

While shepherds watched
Their flocks by night
All seated on the ground
The angel of the Lord came down
And glory shone around
And glory shone around

"Fear not," he said,
For mighty dread
Had seized their troubled minds
"Glad tidings of great joy I bring
To you and all mankind,
To you and all mankind."

"To you in David's
Town this day
Is born of David's line
The Saviour who is Christ the Lord
And this shall be the sign
And this shall be the sign."

"The heavenly Babe
You there shall find
To human view displayed
And meanly wrapped
In swathing bands
And in a manger laid
And in a manger laid."

Thus spake the seraph,
And forthwith
Appeared a shining throng
Of angels praising God, who thus
Addressed their joyful song
Addressed their joyful song

"All glory be to
God on high
And to the earth be peace;
Goodwill henceforth
From heaven to men
Begin and never cease
Begin and never cease!"

A brief history

"While Shepherds Watched Their Flocks" is a traditional and hugely popular Christmas carol, first published in 1700. It's lyrics recount the biblical story of the shepherds who witnessed the angelic announcement of the birth of Jesus Christ. The lyrics draw directly from the Gospel of Luke, capturing their wonder and awe as they receive the news of the Saviour's birth.

Nahum Tate, an Irish poet and playwright, co-wrote the famous Christmas carol with Nicholas Brady. The collaboration between Tate and Brady was part of a larger project: a metrical psalter - a collection of hymns and paraphrased psalms - published in 1700. Tate and Brady were commissioned by the Church of England to provide a version of the Psalms that could be sung more easily than the prose versions commonly used in worship.

The carol was created as part of their efforts to offer a poetic and singable rendition of biblical passages. Tate's motivation, along with Brady, was likely rooted in their desire to enhance the worship experience by providing hymns that were accessible and engaging for congregations.

This endeavour to adapt the Psalms and create new hymns contributed significantly to the English hymnody tradition, leaving a lasting impact on how the Christian community expressed its faith through music.

Nahum Tate's skilful crafting of the lyrics reflects a deep reverence for the sacred account, maintaining a faithful connection to the biblical source. The hymn, through its verses, beautifully portrays the quietude of the nighttime fields, where unsuspecting shepherds become recipients of extraordinary news from the heavenly realm. The poetic rendering captures the awe and wonder experienced by these humble keepers of flocks as the angelic proclamation unfolds before them.

Published during the 18th century, the carol has since become a cherished part of the Christmas musical repertoire, echoing through generations. Its historical significance lies not only in its artistic expression but also in its role as a conduit, transporting listeners back to the hillsides where shepherds were granted a divine revelation. "While Shepherds Watched Their Flocks" invites us to retrace the steps of those shepherds and share in the marvel of the Saviour's birth, fostering a sense of connection with the timeless story of Christmas.

While Tate's primary claim to fame might be his collaboration on the metrical psalter, the enduring popularity of "While Shepherds Watched Their Flocks" ensures his legacy as a contributor to the rich heritage of Christmas carols. The carol is a cherished part of Christmas celebrations, echoing through centuries and resonating with those who seek to connect with the divine during the Advent season.

Unwrapping the story

Throughout each verse, "While Shepherds Watched Their Flocks" transports readers to the Judean hillsides, inviting us to witness a scene of humble shepherds tending their flocks by night. The narrative begins with the shepherds going about their ordinary tasks, unaware that the extraordinary is about to unfold. Suddenly, the heavens burst forth with the glory of the Lord, and an angel appears to deliver the joyous tidings of the Saviour's birth. The hymn captures the essence of this angelic proclamation, recounting the angel's words of peace and goodwill, echoing the biblical message.

As the shepherds hasten to Bethlehem to see the newborn King, the hymn weaves a story of awe and reverence. The imagery of the humble stable and the radiant presence of the Christ child invites people to contemplate the mystery of the Incarnation and the divine in the midst of the ordinary. The hymn's refrain, punctuated by the joyful declaration of "Gloria in excelsis Deo" (Glory to God in the highest), becomes a rhythmic heartbeat throughout. It acts as a rallying cry for singers and listeners to join the heavenly chorus in celebrating the birth of Jesus.

While the hymn centres on the shepherds, it ultimately broadens its scope, encouraging everyone to embrace the timeless message of hope and salvation brought by the Messiah. The shepherds serve as archetypes of all who, like them, respond to the call to seek and worship the Christ child. While Shepherds Watched Their Flocks is as a serene and evocative hymn that captures the simplicity, wonder, and profound implications of the Nativity, inviting us to join in adoration and worship at Christmas.

Morning Devotional

In the quiet embrace of a new day, I gather my thoughts and turn my heart to the timeless message of hope and salvation. May I, like the shepherds of old, respond to the call to seek and embrace the divine presence in the midst of my ordinary life. Grant me the wisdom to recognise moments of grace and the courage to respond with gratitude. In the simplicity of this morning, help me find wonder in the new day and contemplate my journey anchored in the promise of hope.

Evening Devotional

As the day transitions into evening, I reflect on the humble shepherds, finding meaning in their response to the call of worship. In the quiet moments of this night, I acknowledge the message that echoes through the ages - the promise of salvation brought by the Messiah. May my heart be filled with adoration as I recognise the sacred in the ordinary. In this moment of reflection, I offer gratitude for the day's experiences and seek solace in the simplicity of the Nativity story that continues to inspire and guide us.

With Thanks
Tidings of joy to you!

Thank you for taking this journey with us through the world of classic Christmas hymns and carols. We appreciate the time you've spent uncovering some of the stories behind these much loved and timeless musical masterpieces.

It's been a pleasure sharing the rich histories and origins of each carol and we hope this book has added a touch of depth and understanding to your holiday season, allowing you to enjoy these carols with fresh perspectives. Christmas is a time for traditions, and we're grateful to have been a part of yours this year.

As you go about your festive celebrations, whether singing these carols with loved ones or quietly enjoying the tunes in your daily lives, we wish you a season filled with joy, warmth, and moments of reflection. May the spirit of Christmas bring you peace and happiness, and may these carols continue to be a source of happiness, comfort and inspiration.

We also hope you enjoyed the shared moments of reflection and inspiration through the devotional sections of this book. These morning and evening prayers rooted in the themes of the hymns, provide a daily sanctuary for personal contemplation. As you incorporate the words into your routine, may they bring a sense of peace and spiritual grounding to your busy days.

Our aim has been to create a space for you to not only learn about the carols' origins, but also to find peace and understanding in your daily life, allowing a deeper understanding of the season's true significance. We invite you to continue this devotional journey, letting these prayers be a guide for times of quiet thought and spiritual enrichment.

Thank you for allowing us to be a part of your sacred and joyful Advent season.

Printed in Great Britain
by Amazon

49836199R00059